COOKING THE
MICROWAVE
WAY

COOKING THE MICROWAVE WAY

Caroline Ball

This edition produced exclusively for

WHSMITH

COOKING THE
MICROWAVE
WAY

Caroline Ball

This edition produced exclusively for

 WHSMITH

Acknowledgements

The author and publishers would like to thank the following companies for their help in supplying some of the photographs for this book:

Batchelors Foods (pages 101, 138, 178)

Billingtons Sugars (pages 153, 163)

British Bacon Bureau (pages 88, 101, 134, 139)

British Meat (pages 37, 67, 68, 69, 72, 73, 78, 80, 81, 83, 89, 91, 93, 94, 139, 146)

British Sausage Bureau (page 94)

Coates Gaymers Ltd (page 186)

Colman's of Norwich (pages 57, 88, 107)

Danish Agricultural Producers (pages 153, 170)

Dutch Dairy Bureau (pages 40, 42, 43, 46, 47, 86, 107, 112, 148)

Findus Ltd (pages 136, 137)

Green Giant Kitchen (pages 56, 84, 87, 141)

Jif Lemon Bureau (page 171)

Lyons Bakery Ltd (pages 45, 49, 158, 164, 167, 169, 172)

New Zealand Lamb Information Bureau (pages 68, 71, 74, 76, 77, 119)

Pasta Information Centre (pages 112, 113, 115)

Scottish Salmon Information Service (page 61)

Spillers Ltd (pages 59, 144/145, 153, 160)

Jacket and all remaining photography: Paul Williams
Stylist: Penny Markham
Illustrations: Orial Bath

**This edition produced exclusively for
W H Smith**

Published by
Deans International Publishing
52/54 Southwark Street, London SE1 1UA
A division of The Hamlyn Publishing Group Limited
London · New York · Sydney · Toronto

Copyright © The Hamlyn Publishing Group Limited 1983
Reprinted 1984
ISBN 0 603 03109 9

Printed in Italy

Contents

Useful Facts and Figures

Notes on metrication

In this book quantities are given in metric and Imperial measures. Exact conversion from Imperial to metric measures does not usually give very convenient working quantities and so the metric measures have been rounded off into units of 25 grams. The table below shows the recommended equivalents.

Ounces	Approx g to nearest whole figure	Recommended conversion to nearest unit of 25
1	28	25
2	57	50
3	85	75
4	113	100
5	142	150
6	170	175
7	198	200
8	227	225
9	255	250
10	283	275
11	312	300
12	340	350
13	368	375
14	396	400
15	425	425
16 (1 lb)	454	450
17	482	475
18	510	500
19	539	550
20 ($1\frac{1}{4}$ lb)	567	575

Note: When converting quantities over 20 oz first add the appropriate figures in the centre column, then adjust to the nearest unit of 25. As a general guide, 1 kg (1000 g) equals 2.2 lb or about 2 lb 3 oz. This method of conversion gives good results in nearly all cases, although in certain pastry and cake recipes a more accurate conversion is necessary to produce a balanced recipe.

Liquid measures The millilitre has been used in this book and the following table gives a few examples.

Imperial	Approx ml to nearest whole figure	Recommended ml
$\frac{1}{4}$ pint	142	150 ml
$\frac{1}{2}$ pint	283	300 ml
$\frac{3}{4}$ pint	425	450 ml
1 pint	567	600 ml
$1\frac{1}{2}$ pints	851	900 ml
$1\frac{3}{4}$ pints	992	1000 ml (1 litre)

Spoon measures All spoon measures given in this book are level unless otherwise stated.

Can sizes At present, cans are marked with the exact (usually to the nearest whole number) metric equivalent of the Imperial weight of the contents, so we have followed this practice when giving can sizes.

NOTE: **When making any of the recipes in this book, only follow one set of measures as they are not interchangeable.**

Notes for American and Australian users

In America the 8-oz measuring cup is used. In Australia metric measures are now used in conjunction with the standard 250-ml measuring cup. The Imperial pint, used in Britain and Australia, is 20 fl oz, while the American pint is 16 fl oz. It is important to remember that the Australian tablespoon differs from both the British and American tablespoons; the table below gives a comparison. The British standard tablespoon, which has been used throughout this book, holds 17.7 ml, the American 14.2 ml, and the Australian 20 ml. A teaspoon holds approximately 5 ml in all three countries.

British	American	Australian
1 teaspoon	1 teaspoon	1 teaspoon
1 tablespoon	1 tablespoon	1 tablespoon
2 tablespoons	3 tablespoons	2 tablespoons
$3\frac{1}{2}$ tablespoons	4 tablespoons	3 tablespoons
4 tablespoons	5 tablespoons	$3\frac{1}{2}$ tablespoons

An Imperial/American guide to solid and liquid measures

Imperial	American	Imperial	American
Solid measures		**Liquid measures**	
1 lb butter or margarine	2 cups	$\frac{1}{4}$ pint liquid	$\frac{2}{3}$ cup liquid
		$\frac{1}{2}$ pint	$1\frac{1}{4}$ cups
1 lb flour	4 cups	$\frac{3}{4}$ pint	2 cups
1 lb granulated or castor sugar	2 cups	1 pint	$2\frac{1}{2}$ cups
		$1\frac{1}{2}$ pints	$3\frac{3}{4}$ cups
1 lb icing sugar	3 cups	2 pints	5 cups ($2\frac{1}{2}$ pints)
8 oz rice	1 cup		

American terms

The list below gives some American equivalents or substitutes for terms and ingredients used in this book.

British/American
Equipment and terms
deep cake tin/spring form pan
double saucepan/double boiler
flan tin/pie pan
frying pan/skillet
greaseproof paper/wax paper
grill/broil
loaf tin/loaf pan
piping bag/pastry bag
stoned/pitted
Swiss roll tin/jelly roll pan

British/American
Ingredients
aubergine/eggplant
bicarbonate of soda/baking soda
biscuits/crackers, cookies
cocoa powder/unsweetened cocoa
cornflour/cornstarch
courgettes/zucchini
cream, single/cream, light
cream, double/cream, heavy
essence/extract
flour, plain/flour, all-purpose
glacé cherries/candied cherries
icing/frosting
lard/shortening
shortcrust pastry/basic pie dough
spring onion/scallion
sultanas/seedless white raisins
yeast, fresh/yeast, compressed

Introduction

Despite the fact that microwave ovens have been on the domestic scene for many years, there still remains a certain amount of confusion about their workings and, moreover, their use. Novice and experienced cooks alike encounter disappointments and delights with use. It is quite understandable, the microwave oven is a totally new concept in cooking and one that isn't, at first glance, all that easy to understand. The mechanics of microwave cooking are, however, quite simple and, once grasped, open the door to many exciting and memorable meals.

I have set out in this book to clearly explain the mechanics of microwave cooking, recommended procedures to follow to obtain good results and included what I hope are a fair sprinkling of invaluable tips that I have discovered, or have been passed on to me over the years from friends, colleagues and family alike. I hope by following them that you may also enjoy the delights of microwave cooking.

I should like to offer my grateful thanks to Philips Electronics for kindly supplying the microwave oven on which all testing was done for this book.

CAROLINE BALL

MICROWAVE KNOWHOW

The chances are, if you are a busy cook, freezer owner or simply interested in cooking food, you will have studied the possibilities of buying a microwave oven. Tempted by the opportunity to cook, defrost or reheat foods in minutes rather than hours, no one could be surprised at your interest.

Ever since microwave ovens appeared on the scene several years ago, these seemingly 'magical boxes' have aroused interest. But how does the microwave oven cook our food and what makes it so different from conventional cooking? These and many more questions are asked daily in hundreds of department stores throughout the country . . . let's set the record straight:

How Do Microwave Ovens Cook?
The mechanics of microwave cooking are quite simple. Inside the microwave oven is a magnetron vacuum tube. This converts ordinary household electrical energy into high frequency microwaves. These microwaves are absorbed by the moisture in food, causing food molecules to vibrate rapidly and produce heat to cook the food. Since the waves penetrate deeply into the food, the inside starts to cook as well as the outside, and since the molecules are vibrated at many millions of times per second this accounts for the speed of microwave cooking.

Once produced the microwaves can do one of three things:
1) They can be reflected from a surface. Microwaves are reflected by metals — this is why they are safely contained within the metal microwave oven cavity. This also explains why metals cannot be used in the microwave to hold food.
2) Microwaves can pass through substances without changing them. Microwaves will pass through materials like china, glass, pottery, wood etc without heating them. This explains why dishes do not become hot as a result of microwave heating. Dishes only become hot through conduction of heat from food.
3) Finally the microwaves can be absorbed by substances. This is true of foods and the moisture within them. Microwaves cause the molecules in food to literally 'rub shoulders' with one another and the result is intense heat. Such intense heat causes the food to cook.

Are All Microwave Ovens the Same?
At first glance the range of microwave ovens and their features can seem alarming. However, if you study the features they are all basically comprised of the same components — it is only the special additional features that make one microwave different from another.

As you can see from the diagram below the basic unit comprises a door, magnetron, wave stirrer, power supply and controls.

Additional Features
Additional features are numerous and complex and each should be considered fully before investment:

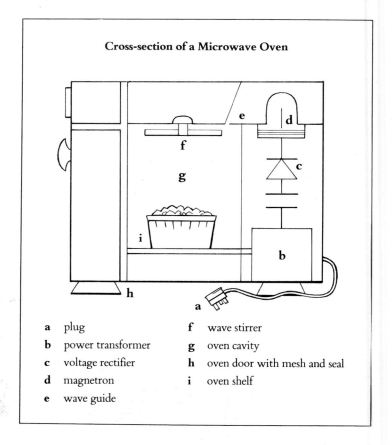

Cross-section of a Microwave Oven

a	plug	f	wave stirrer
b	power transformer	g	oven cavity
c	voltage rectifier	h	oven door with mesh and seal
d	magnetron	i	oven shelf
e	wave guide		

Timer Controls
These are generally standard and are marked in seconds and minutes. Some will however have a numerical mechanical action whilst others will appear digital. Choose the control that you feel happiest observing. The timer will also serve to shut off the microwave energy at the end of the cooking cycle. Choose a model of microwave with a timer control that enables you to set the time accurately.

Cook or Start Control
This cannot be operated until the oven door has been firmly shut and locked into position. This button must also be reactivated should you open the door to check food during the cooking cycle.

On/Off or Power-On Button

Sometimes this is an additional control button to the cook or start control and serves to switch on the fan or interior light to the microwave oven – in other models the cook and start control is incorporated with the on/off or power-on button.

Variable Controls

In much the same way that we have a number of cooking temperatures in the conventional oven for flexibility, microwave ovens have a number of cooking speeds to offer the same. In the microwave oven, variable control means adjusting the output of microwave energy into the microwave cavity. This can effectively slow down or speed up the cooking cycle according to the nature of the food and its characteristics. Variable controls may be described as *Full Power, Medium Power, Defrost Power, Low Power* etc or may be expressed numerically from say 1–10 (*Power 10* being the highest power, referring to cooking on *Full Power*). Variable control ovens some years ago were considered something of a luxury but now are becoming quite standard. At the very least most basic models today incorporate *Full Power* with *Defrost Power* facility for greater cooking choice.

Cooking Guides and Recipe Books

Most manufacturers recognising that microwave cooking is unknown to the majority of purchasers offer a cooking guide on the oven to assist with general cooking procedures. Most will also back up this basic information with a cookery book or guide to getting the best results from the oven. Read the booklet carefully for hints on how to achieve the best results from your particular model with the basic information in this book.

Turntables

Some models incorporate a turntable instead of, or as an extra to the wave stirrer. This ensures even heating of the food. When a turntable is present generally one can forget the need to rotate dishes. Check if your microwave has a fixed or removable turntable. A fixed turntable can restrict the choice of dishes you can use in the oven. Square or rectangular shaped dishes may knock against the sides of the oven and if used for prolonged periods may strain the motor. The best advice is to choose a microwave with a removable turntable or one that can be put out of action when required.

Integral Thermometers or Temperature Probes

These are found on the most advanced microwave ovens and enable you to cook food by the internal temperature of the food, rather than by time. Most probes have a flexible connection to the sides of the oven and can be removed when not in use.

Browning Elements or Integral Grills

Since there is little applied surface heat with microwave cooking, foods cooked in short times do not brown. To overcome this, some models of microwave have browning elements or integral grills fitted into the ceiling of the microwave oven. These grills often act quite independently of the microwave and should be used before or after microwave cooking. Some newer models do however allow you to use the browning element during microwave cooking. The very latest development is a microwave oven that incorporates microwave energy with forced air convection which promotes browning of foods in the short microwave cooking times.

Keep Warm or Stay Hot Controls

These are additional special controls that enable you to keep foods just warm or hot without additional cooking. They use a very low variable control power setting to do this.

Memory Controls

Computer technology has also affected the microwave and now there are memory controls that enable the cook to set varying power settings with different timings for accurate cooking. The microwave will follow such a programme set down in its memory without mechanical adjustment being necessary.

Multiple Level Cooking

This is an exciting new development in the microwave oven. The microwave energy in these ovens is fed into the cavity via the walls rather than from the bottom or top. The energy can be ducted into the varying levels within the oven at different power settings. Such ovens usually have racks or shelving so that you can use the different power settings and cooking speeds to good effect. This means that you could cook foods of totally different natures in the oven at the same time and get good results with all the foods.

Double Oven Microwave Cookers

1   Free Standing

2   Built-in

The Basic Three Types of Microwave Oven

In general terms microwave ovens can be grouped into three basic types – portable, double oven and combination oven microwaves.

Portable Microwave Ovens

These are generally counter top models that simply require a 13-amp or 15-amp plug and socket for use. Using a fixing kit and housing unit, such portable models can also be built-in to work surfaces and kitchen units for a totally integrated look.

Double Oven Microwave Cookers

There are two forms of double oven microwave. The first type is a free-standing cooker with a hob and a microwave oven at eye level and a conventional oven under the hob. The second choice is as a built-in double oven unit, comprising a microwave oven and separate conventional oven with separate hob. The grill in such models is usually incorporated in the top of the conventional oven.

Combination Ovens

These ovens allow you to cook conventionally and by microwave energy together, separately or in sequence according to your needs. Such models usually have a microwave oven output lower than portable or double oven types.

Microwave Procedures and Techniques

In much the same way that we observe cooking procedures in conventional cooking, it is also important to observe some procedures in microwave cooking. Indeed these procedures often take on a new importance because of the speed of microwave cooking. Such techniques as turning over, re-arranging foods and stirring all must be employed carefully to achieve even cooking results. Follow the techniques below in most general cooking uses alongside any special instructions incorporated in the recipes and you will enjoy considerable success:

Turning Foods Over

This is something that we practise every day in conventional cooking to ensure food cooks evenly. The same practise must also be observed in microwave cooking. In most cases, turn the food over halfway through the cooking time unless the recipe instructions specify more regular turning. A fork, pair of tongs or spatula will help in doing this. Turning foods over is generally not a microwave technique applied in isolation it is generally used with the following three techniques, stirring foods, rotating foods or dishes and re-arranging foods.

Stirring Foods

Stirring foods in the microwave must be observed in much the same way as it is used in conventional cooking. However, because microwaves only penetrate foods to a depth of 5 cm (2 inches), stirring is necessary to distribute the heat evenly in microwave cooking. Always stir from the outside of the dish to the centre. The outer edges will always cook or heat faster than the centre which receives less microwave energy. A wooden spoon or spatula is useful in doing this and for short cooking periods may be left in the microwave during cooking.

Rotating Foods or Dishes

When a food cannot be stirred or turned over, it is most important to rotate the food or dish to ensure even cooking. This procedure need not be observed with microwave ovens having a turntable. In most cases a quarter or half-turn halfway through the cooking time is all that is needed.

Turning foods over during cooking is just as important in microwave cooking as conventional cooking for even results. Use a spatula, tongs or a fork.

Stirring foods helps to distribute the heat evenly throughout the cooking period. Stir from the outside of the dish to the centre.

Rotating a dish in the microwave is used when a food cannot be stirred, turned over or re-arranged during cooking. It is also recommended when a microwave does not have a turntable.

To ensure even cooking and defrosting, foods can be re-arranged in the dish during the cooking or defrosting time.

Covering foods during cooking speeds up cooking times and holds in moisture. A tight-fitting lid, cooking bag, cling film and greaseproof paper will all prove useful covers.

Re-arranging Foods

Another way of ensuring that food cooks, reheats or defrosts evenly is to re-arrange the food during cooking. No microwave has a perfectly tuned energy pattern and most microwave owners will experience hot or cool spots in their ovens – re-arranging foods during the cooking time overcomes such 'blackspot' areas and ensures even results.

Covering Foods

If you cover a food during microwave cooking you effectively speed up the cooking time, hold in the moisture and also prevent spattering on the oven walls and therefore save yourself from unnecessary cleaning.

There are several ways in which you can effectively cover foods during microwave cooking. A tight-fitting lid to a dish is probably the most obvious but if you are using a dish without a lid try placing a saucer over the dish to substitute a lid. Plastic cook-in bags or roaster bags are also good covers especially for cooking vegetables and roasts. Remember to replace any metal ties with rubber bands or string. Absorbent kitchen towel is another useful cover especially in covering fatty foods like bacon or those with a lot of moisture like jacket potatoes. If the dish is of an unusual shape or if the food protrudes above the dish in an irregular way then greaseproof paper or cling film will prove useful covers since they mould to the contents readily. Secure any greaseproof paper with string around the dish or tuck under the base.

Removing Excess Cooking Juices

Any juices that are produced during microwave cooking will continue to attract microwave energy and can

Cooking juices attract microwave energy, leaving less to cook the food itself – for extra fast cooking times remove excess juices with a baster during cooking.

Some liquids and fatty foods spatter during cooking – absorbent kitchen towel if placed over the food prevents spattering on the oven walls.

in effect slow down the cooking process. Remove any juices at regular intervals during the cooking time with a bulb baster. If the food starts to dry out towards the latter stages of the cooking time, these juices can always be re-introduced.

Drying Techniques

In many ways the microwave simulates a steam cabinet and does not produce crisp or dry results. Absorbent kitchen towel is one of the most useful materials that you can use to overcome this. Place jacket potatoes on a double-thickness of absorbent kitchen towel and they will cook dry and crisp. Bacon if covered with or placed between two sheets of absorbent kitchen towel will also cook dry and crisp rather than greasy or soggy. The same technique can also be used to dry herbs or flowers in the microwave. Place the chosen herbs between two pieces of absorbent kitchen towel and cook until the herbs are dry enough to crumble. The same practice can also be used to dry flowers.

Releasing Pressure in Foods

Any foods that have a tight-fitting skin or membrane must be pricked prior to cooking in the microwave. Failure to do so will inevitably cause bursting or exploding as the pressure mounts during the cooking from the production of steam. The same procedure must be observed when using cook-in bags, boil-in-the-bag pouches and roaster bags. Always prick cling film or pierce in a couple of places if using as a cover for a dish.

This technique must also be used when cooking whole eggs – microwave energy is attracted to the fats in the egg yolk and therefore the yolk cooks faster than the white. Prick the yolk carefully with a cocktail stick or the tip of a knife to ensure that the yolk does not explode.

Shielding Foods

Shielding is a technique employed to protect vulnerable parts of a food from over-cooking. The sorts of sensitive areas that are prone to overcooking include the breasts, wing tips, drumsticks and tail-end of poultry, the heads and tails of fish, the thinner end of a leg of lamb, the inside edge of a pastry flan and any fatty areas of food, like the fatty rind of a piece of bacon, pork or ham. To shield these areas from microwave energy it is recommended that small strips of foil are used to cover the sensitive parts. This is the only time when small pieces of foil are generally permissible within the microwave oven. Wrap the foil around the affected part or secure to the food with cocktail sticks. Add the foil either prior to cooking and remove halfway through the cooking time or add as the areas seem to be just cooked.

A piece of absorbent towel will absorb excess moisture. To dry herbs, place between two sheets of towel and cook until they are dry and can be crumbled.

To relieve the pressure and steam that builds up during microwave cooking, foods with skins or membranes and boil-in-bag pouches need to be pricked or pierced before cooking.

Shielding sensitive parts of foods with small pieces of foil is permissible. Sensitive areas include poultry breasts, wing tips and drumsticks, fish heads and tails and the thin end of a leg of lamb.

A roasting rack is a useful piece of equipment for raising foods above their juices during cooking. The same rack is useful for reheating bread rolls so that they stay dry and crisp.

Foods continue to cook in the microwave when the energy is turned off through conduction. Cover foods with foil to make full use of this time.

Observing Standing Times

Foods cooked in the microwave will continue to cook after the microwave energy has been turned off. This cooking continues because of conduction of heat within the food. It is important to observe this standing time to make full use of the microwave energy by ensuring that you do not cook the foods too much — otherwise upon standing the foods may overcook. A typical example of this is with cooking cakes. When cooked sufficiently most cakes will still appear to have a moist surface. Upon observing the standing time this crust will dry out and cook with the conducted heat in the cake. Always err on the side of safety with cooking times — it is easy to add extra cooking time but impossible to ever take it away!

For foods that need to be served hot this standing time is best carried out under foil. The foil will keep the heat trapped inside the food, keeping it hot enough to serve without reheating. Observing this standing time with roasts will also mean they are easier to carve since the muscle meat fibres relax after cooking.

Cooking with a Microwave Thermometer

A lot of the guesswork with microwave cooking can be erased with the use of a specially designed microwave thermometer. A thermometer will tell you at a glance whether the food is cooked or not by recording at eye level the internal temperature of the food. Follow the instructions below for inserting a thermometer into a roast.

A sophisticated version of the thermometer is a temperature probe (see page 27). This feature is often incorporated with a memory device within the oven which is programmed to recall the internal temperatures of literally hundreds of foods when cooked.

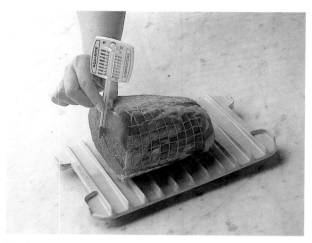

To insert a microwave thermometer, measure the distance from the outside of the meat to the centre of the thickest muscle with your fingers. Mark the point where the sensor touches the edge of the roast.

Insert the thermometer to the depth marked by your fingers. Select an angle which will place the top of the sensor in the centre of the meaty area, not touching fat or bone.

Arranging Foods in the Microwave

In just the same way as we arrange food for even cooking in the conventional oven or under the conventional grill, we must arrange food carefully in the microwave oven to achieve even cooking. If you are cooking several items of the same food then arrange these in a ring pattern on the base of the oven or in a dish. A ring pattern is recommended because the centre of a dish receives less energy than the edges which all receive equal amounts.

Any irregular-shaped foods like chicken drumsticks, broccoli, chops or whole fish should also be positioned to take into account this action. Always make sure that the foods are positioned so that the thicker meatier parts of the foods are at the edge of the dish where they will receive most energy and that the thinner portions are pointing to the centre where they will receive less.

Since some foods are more vulnerable to cooking by microwave, we must also arrange them in such a way to make best use of the energy. Bury these foods – which include cheese and meat – attracting microwave energy deep into the dish; or cover them with a sauce so that they do not overcook while the remaining ingredients stay undercooked or even raw.

Factors Which Affect Microwave Cooking

Density of the Food

The denser a food is, the longer it will take to cook. For example a piece of meat the same size as a large cake will take much longer to cook or defrost despite its identical size. For this reason, light porous foods like cakes, biscuits, breads and puddings will cook much faster than meats, vegetables and dense pasta dishes. When cooking a dish that has both dense and light structured foods, place the denser foods to the outer edge of the dish where they will receive the maximum amount of energy and the lighter porous foods in the centre where they receive less.

Starting Temperature of the Food

The colder the temperature of the food the longer it will take to cook. Adjust the times in the recipes according to whether your ingredients are at room temperature, chilled or even lightly-frozen. All the times given in the recipes refer to foods cooked from room temperature unless otherwise stated.

When cooking frozen foods, always defrost first for good results unless the recipe instructions specify otherwise.

Size of the Food

Because microwaves only penetrate to a depth of about 5 cm (2 inches) it follows that larger pieces of food will take longer to cook than smaller pieces. Wherever possible make sure the pieces are of a uniform size for good even cooking results.

If you are cooking several items of the same food, arrange in a ring pattern for even results. The centre receives less microwave energy while the sides receive equal amounts.

Unevenly-shaped foods like chicken drumsticks and broccoli should be placed with the thinner parts to the centre where they will receive less energy for even cooking results.

Shape of the Food

Most foods have an irregular shape, for example, chops, chicken drumsticks, joints of meat etc. Wherever possible try and secure foods into regular shapes for microwave cooking. Where this is not possible then remember to place the larger, denser portions of the food to the outer edge of the dish, leaving the thinner and smaller portions in the centre or shield the thinner, smaller and therefore more vulnerable areas with small pieces of foil.

Quantity of Food

Timings in the microwave oven are directly related to the quantity of food being cooked. For example two jacket potatoes will take almost twice as long to cook as one jacket potato. Unfortunately the relationship isn't quite that simple otherwise cooking times would be easy to calculate – as a general guideline if you double the amount of food being cooked in the microwave you should increase the cooking time by about one half. Err on the side of safety until you get to know your own microwave oven and its speed of cooking.

Composition of the Food

Fats and sugars absorb microwave energy and attract the energy more than other liquids and components. This means that foods with a high sugar or fat content will generally cook faster than those that have not. Foods with a low moisture content also cook faster than wetter mixtures of the same shape, density and size.

Bones in Meat

Bone conducts heat into food, therefore the food next to the bone will generally cook faster than the remaining meat. To achieve even cooking results it is recommended that wherever possible meats should be boned and rolled to a uniform shape. If boning is not possible then shield the area next to the bone with foil to prevent over-cooking about halfway through the cooking time.

Position of Food in the Oven

Any foods that are nearer to the energy source of an oven will cook faster than those that are further away – this is true in both microwave and conventional cooking. For even cooking, turn foods over, re-arrange or stir during the cooking time to take into account this action.

The Question of Browning

There are some disadvantages to microwave cooking, the most obvious being browning. Since there is no applied surface heat, food does not brown readily on the outside of food with short cooking times. A large turkey cooked in the microwave will brown without any special treatment due to its long cooking time, but steaks, chops and small roasts may well look unappetisingly grey.

There are a good many ways to overcome this with meat and poultry dishes:

★ Manufacturers now have microwave models with integral browning elements or grills that are incorporated in the roof of the oven. These can be used in some cases prior to cooking, after cooking or in special cases during cooking depending upon the type – check the individual manufacturers instructions. The same effect can however be achieved with a conventional grill.

★ There are several microwave browning dishes on the market which all assist with pre-browning meat, poultry and fish prior to microwave cooking. The same browning dish can also be used to brown and 'fry' sandwiches and eggs.

★ Some manufacturers have also now introduced special browning agents and mixes to coat meat, fish and poultry prior to cooking. These are usually dark coloured marinade type sauces which you brush on the food or there are dark coloured spicy mixtures to coat the food.

★ Home-made browning agents that work very well include coating foods with browned breadcrumbs, dusting with ground paprika pepper, coating with a colourful dry soup mix, brushing with tomato or brown sauce, coating with crushed crisps or brushing with soy sauce.

Browning is not just a problem associated with meats and poultry but also with cakes, biscuits and breads. Choosing a dark coloured mixture helps – like chocolate, ginger, coffee or spice, but if you wish to have a plain cake or biscuit mixture then the following tips to overcome the pale appearance may prove useful:

* Try sprinkling cakes and biscuits with chopped nuts, a mixture of cinnamon and sugar, mixed chopped glacé fruits, toasted coconut, hundreds and thousands or chocolate vermicelli before cooking.

* A colourful frosting or icing on a cake after cooking will quickly hide any pale, uncooked-looking crust.

It is very easy to disguise the pale crust of a microwave baked bread:

* Quickly brown under a preheated hot grill after microwave cooking.

* Try sprinkling bread loaves and rolls with poppy seeds, cracked wheat, buckwheat, grated cheese, toasted sesame seeds, chopped nuts, caraway seeds or dried herbs prior to cooking – they all give an interesting crust to the bread.

The pale unbrowned crust of a cake can be improved by sprinkling with vermicelli, cinnamon and sugar, chopped nuts, glacé fruits or toasted coconut prior to cooking or iced after cooking.

Breads do not brown with microwave cooking. For colour and texture sprinkle with chopped nuts, toasted sesame seeds, poppy seeds, buckwheat, caraway seeds or dried herbs before cooking.

Some foods like chicken drumsticks benefit from the use of browning aids – try coating chicken pieces with tomato sauce, crushed crisps, a dry soup mix, butter and paprika, breadcrumbs or a whole chicken with soy sauce.

Good results can be obtained for browning traditionally grilled foods like chops by cooking them on a microwave browning dish. Follow the manufacturer's instructions.

When defrosting foods frozen in a block, break away the defrosted pieces as they thaw allowing the energy to concentrate on the unfrozen block.

For even defrosting turn foods over, wherever possible, halfway through the defrosting time.

Where turning over and breaking up is not possible during defrosting, rotate the food for even thawing results.

Defrosting Foods

The microwave has often been given the title the unfreezer since it efficiently defrosts foods in a fraction of the time it normally takes at room temperature. Most microwave ovens, recognising this special action, have a *Defrost Power* facility on the control dial. If your oven does not have a *Defrost Power* button then you can simulate this by turning the oven on and off at regular intervals until the frozen food is defrosted. The *Defrost Power* facility simply automates this switching on and off.

When defrosting foods refer to the times in the chart on page 22 but always err on the side of safety by under rather than over timing until you can readily judge the cooking or defrosting speeds of your microwave.

The following hints will also ensure good even defrosting:

★ Pierce any skins, membranes or pouches before defrosting

★ Remove any metal containers, ties or dishes before defrosting

★ Turn foods over during defrosting

★ If turning foods over during defrosting is not possible then rotate the dish to ensure even heating

★ Flex any pouches that cannot be broken up or stirred during the defrosting time and rotate on a regular basis

★ Place any foods like cakes, bread rolls, sausage rolls and pastry items on a double sheet of absorbent kitchen towel when defrosting to absorb any excess moisture

★ Any blocks of frozen food should be broken up with a fork during defrosting so that the microwave energy can concentrate on the unfrozen block

★ Separate any blocks of frozen meats like hamburgers, sausages and steaks as they defrost

★ Remove any giblets from the cavity of chickens and other game or poultry meats as they defrost

★ Open all cartons and remove any lids before defrosting

★ Remove any thaw juices or drips from frozen foods during the defrosting time with a bulb baster – these will only continue to attract microwave energy leaving less to defrost the main food

★ With items like meat joints, whole poultry birds and whole fish defrost the items until icy then leave to completely defrost at room temperature

★ If any parts of the food start to defrost at too fast a rate or even start to cook or become warm, then shield or protect these areas with small strips of foil. These can be attached with wooden cocktail sticks where necessary

★ Always observe a standing time action – foods will continue to thaw with the heat produced via conduction. Allow foods to defrost until just icy for best results

Reheating Foods

Dried-up meals should become a thing of the past with the use of the microwave oven. Dishes can quickly be reheated without fear of drying out to just-cooked freshness. For best results follow the guidelines below and the chart on page 23:

★ Arrange foods on the plate when reheating so that the thicker denser and meatier portions are to the outer edge of the dish, where they will receive the maximum amount of energy, and leave the thinner areas to the centre where they will receive less

★ Cover foods when reheating with a layer of cling film to retain moisture

★ When reheating observe the standing time recommended in cooking procedures to make maximum use of the microwave energy and to prevent overcooking of the reheated dish

★ The times in the reheating chart refer to foods at room temperature. Allow extra time if the food is chilled

★ When plating up meals for reheating, try and make sure that the food is arranged in an even layer

★ When reheating potatoes in their jackets, breads, pastries or moist foods, place them on a sheet of absorbent kitchen towel so that it may absorb the moisture during the reheating time

★ If you are in any doubt about a food losing moisture during reheating then wrap the food in a tight skin of cling film. Remember to pierce the cling film in a couple of places first

★ Stir foods regularly during the reheating process. If stirring is not possible then rotate the food or dish or re-arrange during the reheating time

If some areas of food start to defrost too quickly, become too warm or even start to cook during defrosting, shield with small pieces of foil.

When heating plated meals, arrange thick areas and dense foods to the outside of the dish, with easy-to-heat foods on the inside.

For even defrosting and heating in one operation, stir defrosted food from the outside to the centre of the dish, once or twice during the cooking time.

Guide to defrosting

Throughout the recipe sections in this book you will find advice on how to defrost and cook basic foods. To defrost and cook ready-prepared foods follow the instructions and times in the chart below:

Food	Quantity or Weight	Defrosting time and power setting	Special instructions
Meats			
Meat casserole	per 675 g/1½ lb	8–10 minutes on **Medium power** then 5–8 on **Full power**	Separate any meat pieces with a fork after about 5 minutes.
Roast beef and gravy	per 350 g/12 oz	3 minutes on **Full power**, allow to stand for 3 minutes then a further 3½ minutes on **Full power**	
Shepherd's pie	400 g/14 oz	5 minutes on **Full power**, allow to stand for 2 minutes then a further 6 minutes on **Full power**	Remove from foil tray if necessary.
Soups			
Home-made soups	per 1 litre/2 pints (U.S. 5 cups)	18 minutes on **Full power**	
Fish			
Buttered kipper fillets	175 g/6 oz	5 minutes on **Full power**	Pierce the boil-in-bag prior to cooking
Cod in Sauce	175 g/6 oz	5½ minutes on **Full power**	Pierce the boil-in-bag prior to cooking
Fish cakes	2 (50 g/2 oz) cakes	2½ minutes on **Full power**, allow to stand for 3 minutes then a further 1 minute on **Full power**	
Prawns	per 450 g/1 lb	4 minutes on **Defrost power**	Break up with a fork halfway through the defrosting time.
Crabmeat	per 225 g/8 oz	3–4 minutes on **Defrost power**	Break up with a fork after 2 minutes.
Cakes and Desserts			
Cheesecake	1 (20-cm/8-inch)	1½ minutes on **Full power**, allow to stand for 15 minutes	Remove any foil packaging.
Cream sponge	1 (18-cm/7-inch)	¾ minute on **Full power**, allow to stand for 5 minutes	
Mousse tubs	1	¼ minute on **Full power**, allow to stand for 5 minutes	Remove the lid prior to heating.
Cream éclairs	4	¾ minute on **Full power**, allow to stand for 10 minutes	
Cream doughnuts	3	½ minute on **Full power**, allow to stand for 10 minutes	
Jam doughnuts	2	1½ minutes on **Full power**, allow to stand for 5 minutes	
Miscellaneous			
Puff pastry	400 g/14 oz	2 minutes on **Full power**, allow to stand for 5 minutes	
Shortcrust pastry	400 g/14 oz	2 minutes on **Full power**, allow to stand for 5 minutes	
Pizza	1 large to serve 2–3	4 minutes on **Full power**	
Bread	1 large loaf	2 minutes on **Full power**, allow to stand for 6 minutes then a further 2 minutes on **Full power**	
Cooked rice	450 g/1 lb	8 minutes on **Full power**	Pierce any cooking bag if used.

Guide to reheating

Food	Quantity or Weight	Reheating time and power setting
Meats		
Main dishes with sauce	1 serving	3 minutes on **Full power**
	2 servings	6 minutes on **Full power**
	4 servings	10 minutes on **Full power**
Plated meals – meat and two vegetables	1 serving	6 minutes on **Full power**
Hamburgers	1 serving	1 minute on **Full power**
	2 servings	$1\frac{1}{2}$–2 minutes on **Full power**
	4 servings	$2\frac{1}{2}$–3 minutes on **Full power**
Hot dogs and frankfurters	1 serving	$\frac{1}{2}$ minute on **Full power**
	2 servings	1 minute on **Full power**
	4 servings	$1\frac{1}{2}$ minutes on **Full power**
Sliced chicken or meat	1 serving	$1\frac{1}{2}$–2 minutes on **Medium power**
	2 servings	$2\frac{1}{2}$–$3\frac{1}{2}$ minutes on **Medium power**
Soups		
	1 serving	2 minutes on **Full power**
	2 servings	3–4 minutes on **Full power**
Fish		
Fish in sauce	1 serving	2 minutes on **Full power**
	2 servings	3–$3\frac{1}{2}$ minutes on **Full power**
Vegetables		
	1 serving	1 minute on **Full power**
	2 servings	2 minutes on **Full power**
	4 servings	4 minutes on **Full power**
Stewed Fruit		
	1 serving	1 minute on **Full power**
	2 servings	$1\frac{1}{2}$–2 minutes on **Full power**
	4 servings	3–4 minutes on **Full power**
Puddings and Desserts		
Sponge pudding	1 serving	$\frac{1}{2}$ minute on **Full power**
Milk pudding	1 serving	1 minute on **Full power**
Fruit pie	1 serving	$\frac{1}{2}$ minute on **Full power**
Miscellaneous		
Rice and pasta	1 serving	$\frac{1}{2}$–1 minute on **Full power**
	2 servings	1–2 minutes on **Full power**
Porridge	1 serving	1–2 minutes on **Full power**
	2 servings	2–3 minutes on **Full power**
Baked beans	1 serving	$1\frac{1}{2}$–2 minutes on **Full power**
	2 servings	$2\frac{1}{2}$–3 minutes on **Full power**
Sauces	300 ml/$\frac{1}{2}$ pint (U.S. $1\frac{1}{4}$ cups)	2–3 minutes on **Full power**

Dishes For Microwave Cooking

Microwaves are either reflected by, passed through, or absorbed by different materials – hence the need to adapt cooking utensils for microwave oven use. Generally speaking, the range of cooking utensils that can be used in the microwave is wider than those that can be used in the conventional oven. Serving dishes, glass, china, pottery, paper, linen, basketware and some plastics that could not be used in the conventional oven now find a place within the microwave.

There are however a few exceptions. Most manufacturers object to the use of metal. Metal present in the oven will reflect the microwaves so they will not penetrate the food to be cooked. So this means goodbye to those handy metal foil dishes for use in the freezer, baking trays, cast-iron casseroles, porcelain-coated metal containers, plates and dishes trimmed with metallic designs, any dish with a metal screw or handle and paper-coated metal ties for use with freezer and roasting bags – although they are easily replaced with elastic bands or string. Indeed if you do use large amounts of metal in the microwave you could damage the magnetron. Follow the instructions given for testing a dish for microwave use, opposite.

It isn't only important to consider the material of the dish but also the shape for suitability in the microwave. Round and ring shapes give the best results. Ring shapes especially, since microwaves only penetrate to a depth of about 5 cm (2 inches). For the same reason shallow dishes also prove better dishes than deeper ones. Square, oval and rectangular shapes are less efficient since the energy seems to concentrate in the corners. To prevent over-cooking when using such dishes, protect or shield the corners half-way through the cooking time with small pieces of foil. The final guideline is to try and use a dish which has straight sides rather than curved – the microwaves penetrate the straight sides much more evenly giving good cooking or reheating results.

Metal skewers may be used in the microwave providing they have wooden handles and the food is packed tightly together leaving no metal exposed. Indeed if you make sure that the amount of metal exposed is far less than the area of food you can even use some skewers with metal handles. The obvious solution, of course, is to replace all metal skewers with disposable wooden ones that are now available in most department stores.

Glass, Pottery and China

Most people have a good selection of glass, both ovenproof and plain, pottery and china and all can be put to good use in the microwave oven for cooking and reheating purposes. Check that the dishes do not have a metallic trim, screws or handles that are screwed or glued on and that the pottery dish is non-porous.

The exception is a chicken brick or porous baking brick. This can be used very successfully in the microwave for slow-cooking meats, fish and poultry. The microwave energy is attracted to the moisture held in the clay rather than the food – so a slower, more gentle cooking action is produced. Soak the clay brick in cold water for about 15 minutes before use. Add the food and cook until the food is tender. Since the energy is attracted to the moisture in the pots these dishes, unlike others, do become very hot during cooking so take care to use ovenproof gloves when removing from the oven, and take extra care when lifting the lid since a great deal of steam is often produced.

Paper

Paper can be used most effectively in the microwave for quick cooking and speedy reheating. Many manufacturers have brought out ranges made of sturdy paper especially for microwave oven use. The ranges consist of plates, cups, plated meal dishes and shallow cooking dishes. Since paper is generally porous it is not recommended for long cooking periods in the microwave or for use with dishes that have a high sugar or water content. Perhaps its most useful role is in covering foods during microwave cooking. Absorbent kitchen paper towel placed over fatty foods or those that tend to spatter keeps the oven walls clean. Paper will also prove invaluable for drying herbs. Paper will also find a use in absorbing excess water during cooking. Jacket potatoes for example, placed on a sheet of paper will cook more crisp and dry rather than having soggy bottoms.

Paper or cardboard boxes will also prove useful in duplicating the role of traditional metal baking or cake tins if lined with cling film or greaseproof paper

Paper napkins also have their use for holding bread rolls or biscuits when quickly reheating or warming prior to serving.

Wax-coated paper plates and cups should not be used since the high temperatures in foods will often cause the wax to melt. They can however be used to defrost foods where temperatures are very low.

Cotton and Linen Napkins

Cotton and linen napkins can be used to reheat bread rolls or pastries in the microwave – where short cooking times are employed. Do check that the napkins are either 100% cotton or linen and that they do not contain any synthetic fibres. If in any doubt do not use.

Straw and Wood

Just like cotton and linen these can also be used for short cooking or reheating times in the microwave. They are useful for reheating bread rolls in baskets, stirring sauces and mixtures as wooden spoons or quick reheating or warming in bowls. If the materials are used for longer cooking times then the straw or wood is likely to char or crack.

Plastics

The only reliable indicator to look out for with plastics for microwave use is 'dishwasher safe'. This generally implies that the plastic is a hard thermoplastic that will withstand reasonably high temperatures. Softer plastics can however be used for short cooking times and where the food does not have a high sugar or fat content that will heat to very high temperatures.

Plastic bags, boil-in-bags, roaster bags and cling film are all useful plastics for microwave use. Remember however with plastic bags to pierce the bags before use to allow any steam to escape during cooking. Replace any metal ties with rubber bands or string too – although most manufacturers are now supplying bags with plastic ties for microwave use.

Plastic foam cups and plastic baby bottles are also suitable for microwave use when short cooking or heating times are employed.

Do not use melamine in the microwave – it absorbs enough microwave energy to cause charring or burning which is irreversible.

Ring moulds are ideal for cooking cakes, breads and meatloaves. To make your own, simply place a glass tumbler in the centre of a round dish and hold down while adding the mixture.

Microwave energy is often concentrated in the corners of rectangular and square dishes. Protect and shield the corners with small strips of foil to prevent overcooking in these areas.

To test if a dish is suitable for microwave use. Place 250 ml/8 fl oz (U.S. 1 cup) water in a glass jug in the dish. Cook 1 minute on Full Power. If water becomes hot the dish can be used. If dish becomes hot it cannot.

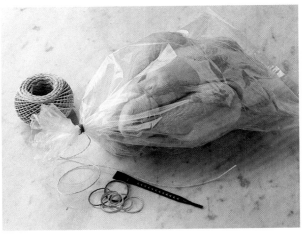

Do not use metal in the microwave unless specified. Replace metal ties for roasting bags with string or rubber bands and use wooden kebab skewers wherever possible.

Microwave Cookware

Recognising the need for certain special pieces of equipment for microwave use, several manufacturers are now making ranges of special microwave cookware. These have been specially designed for microwave use and are generally made of a thermoplastic. Some ranges can also be used in the conventional oven up to certain moderate temperatures. With continued microwave success the range of dishes is expanding from the general cooking dishes to ring moulds, roasting racks and trays, bun or muffin trays, bacon racks, casseroles or cake moulds, savarin moulds and microwave saucepans. A basic selection is really worth the initial investment especially since some can also be used in the freezer – a bonus when that means you can freeze, cook and serve in the same dish!

Microwave Thermometers

Ordinary mercury thermometers cannot be used in the microwave oven. For this reason special microwave thermometers have been developed for use in cooking meats, poultry, fish and preserves in the microwave. Most are made of a thermoplastic that will withstand the high temperatures associated with jam and sweet making but do check the manufacturers instructions for use. See page 16 for instructions on how to insert a meat thermometer for good cooking results.

Roasting Bags

I have enjoyed considerable success using roasting bags for cooking meat and poultry in the microwave oven. The bags seem to encourage browning of the meat or poultry and when used in conjunction with a browning aid the meat or poultry seems to brown as readily as with conventional cooking. Remember to substitute any metal ties with elastic bands or string.

To enjoy really good roasting results place the meat or poultry roast on an upturned saucer or on a roasting rack inside the roasting bag. This ensures that the roast is elevated out of the cooking juices so that it really does roast rather than stew.

Microwave Separating Rings

These are rings of thermoplastic that are used to separate plates when cooking or reheating plated meals of food in the microwave. In effect they enable you to stack food or dishes in the microwave oven.

Defrost Boxes

These are plastic see-through boxes that enable you to place a food item on a tray within a box in the microwave for efficient defrosting. Any juices resulting from thawing are collected in the base. The defrost box also doubles as a useful roasting rack with cover and storage box for refrigerator use.

Microwave Ladles, Tongs, Stirrers and Fish Slice

Specially produced in a thermoplastic these utensils can be left in the microwave during cooking operations since they will withstand microwave energy and the temperatures produced in normal cooking. Always check when leaving such items in the oven that they do not restrict any turntable action by catching on the walls or ceiling – if they do they can strain the turntable motor.

Independent Microwave Turntable

Many microwave ovens do not have a turntable. Often these are not necessary if rotating of dishes is employed. Turntables are however a useful feature when even cooking is very important, as in cooking cakes and breads. For this reason one manufacturer has now developed an independent microwave turntable with motor for use in those microwave ovens that do not have a fixed turntable feature. Made of thermoplastic you simply place it in the base of the oven and switch on when required. The motor will work for up to about $1\frac{1}{2}$ hours before needing a recharge – remembering that $1\frac{1}{2}$ hours is a long time in microwave terms. The microwave turntable comes complete with a battery recharger to work the motor.

Specialist Microwave Equipment

Alongside and in line with new developments in microwave cooking have come a number of specialist microwave cooking utensils. Many of these have been developed in the USA but are quickly finding world-wide distribution:

Temperature Probe

Perhaps the most popular new fixed feature in micro-wave ovens is a temperature probe. This is usually attached, via a socket, to the side of the oven and generally is removable. A temperature probe is rather like a thermometer, it enables you to cook foods by temperature rather than by time – you simply set the internal temperature required to cook the food and when that temperature is reached the oven simply switches itself off. The skill in using a probe is not in knowing the internal temperatures required, a guide is usually given by the manufacturer, but in positioning the probe accurately in the food. Follow the guidelines for positioning a thermometer and you can't go far wrong. Generally a probe is positioned in the thickest or densest part of the food or dish. It is a good feature to look out for and a testing method to use along with others for never-fail results.

Browning Dishes

There are a variety of browning dishes on the market ranging from the small brown n' sear dishes to the larger browning griddles – they are all made from the same glass-ceramic substance that has a special coating which attracts and absorbs microwave energy. Browning dishes are simple to use – preheat the dish according to the manufacturers' instructions, usually about 5 min-utes. Add the food and quickly turn on all sides to brown. Continue cooking according to the recipe instructions.

Browning dishes are especially useful for browning meat and poultry joints, small meat and poultry cuts, vegetables, sandwiches, fish and 'frying' eggs.

If you are cooking a roast or dish where a lot of cooking juices are expected then look out for a browning dish with a well around the outside to collect the drippings. This will also mean the food crisps better rather than stews in its own juices.

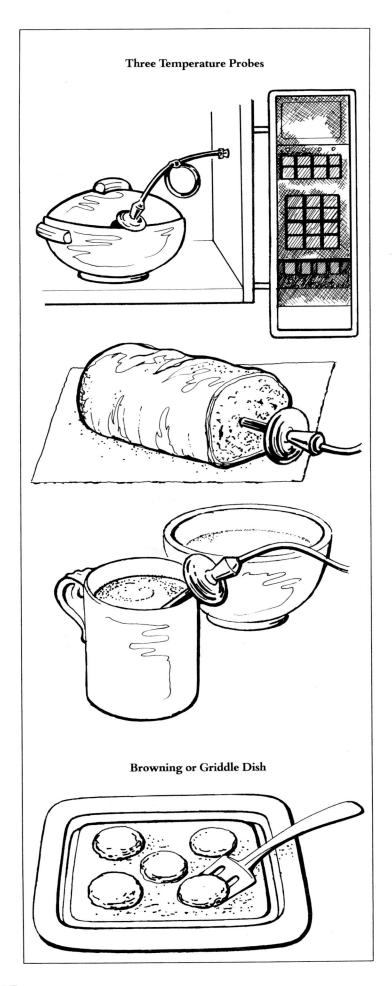

Three Temperature Probes

Browning or Griddle Dish

Bacon Tree

An ingenious new device this really is a development from the bacon rack. Made from microwave-proof material, a bacon tree raises bacon above its own juices during cooking for extra crisp results. Most bacon trees hold up to 6–8 slices and some come complete with a small dish to collect drippings.

Cupcaker

The cupcaker combines together two principles for cooking individual cup cakes to achieve perfect results. It arranges cup cakes in a ring shape for even cooking and has holes pierced in the base to allow the easy escape of steam during the cooking operation. Made of a microwave-proof thermoplastic, it can be used to cook stuffing balls and eggs if the bases are lined with cling film.

Microwave Trivet

Available on its own or with an integral plastic dish, a microwave trivet acts like a conventional roasting rack, holding meat above its juices to prevent stewing. Made of thermoplastic material, ideal for microwave oven use, it is also useful for heating and warming bread rolls.

Bacon Tree

Cupcaker

Trivet or Roasting Racks

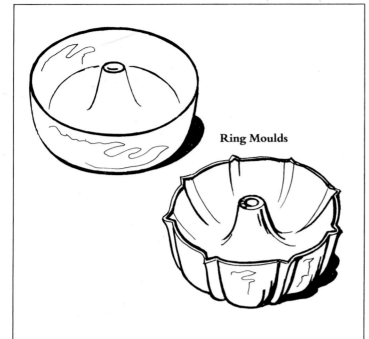

Ring Moulds

Chicken Roast and Saver

Ring Moulds

Since microwaves generally only penetrate to a depth of about 5 cm (2 inches), ring-shaped moulds are ideal for cooking cakes, quick breads, meat loaves and puddings in the minimum time on *Full Power*. There are a wide selection available for microwave use, both fluted and straight-sided, to give attractive results.

Chicken Roast and Saver

This is a specialist piece of microwave equipment incorporating a microwave trivet and cover for cooking poultry and meat. The trivet raises the meat above its juices during cooking, the base collects the drippings for making gravy and the lid prevents spatterings from collecting on the oven walls as well as being an effective storage cover. Some makes can be used in the conventional oven up to 180°C (350°F) too.

Microwave Saucepans

Looking just like and useful in the same way as conventional saucepans, microwave saucepans are made of a microwave-proof thermoplastic rather than metal. They are available in a fairly comprehensive range of sizes from 600 ml/1 pint (U.S. $2\frac{1}{2}$ cups) to 1.75 litres/3 pints (U.S. 7 cups).

Microwave Egg and Cake Rings

Looking very much like muffin rings, microwave egg and cake rings are small rings made of microwave-proof thermoplastic that are ideal for cooking individual cakes, eggs, stuffing balls and any mixture that requires a ring-shape during cooking. The rings should be placed on a microwave tray or plate before filling.

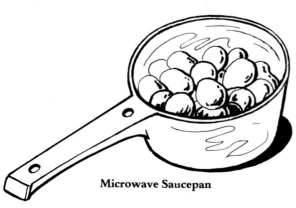

Microwave Saucepan

Egg and Cake Rings

What Does a Microwave Oven Offer?

Speed
You can save up to 75% of normal cooking time with the use of a microwave oven in your kitchen.

Money
Since the microwave does not have a lengthy heating up period, cooks for a shorter time and requires less energy it follows that you will save money on energy bills.

No Cooking Smells
Cooking odours are generally contained within the microwave cavity so cooking odours are kept to the very minimum.

A Cool Kitchen
Because of the mechanics of microwave cooking, the microwave oven, its dishes and the kitchen all stay cool – only food is cooked to piping hot.

Less Risk of Burns
Since dishes do not become hot through microwave cooking only through conduction of heat from foods there is less risk of getting a nasty burn from dishes or from the oven itself.

Less Washing Up
It is possible to cook and serve in the same container with microwave cooking thereby reducing the amount of washing up. Washing up also proves easier since there is little baked-on food.

The End to Dried Out Dinners
Everyone seems to have experienced a dried out, curled up dinner or meal because they have been late. Such meals should become a thing of the past since the microwave enables you to reheat meals in seconds without drying out.

Good Nutritional Values in Foods
Nutritional loss in foods is often associated with overcooking. Since the timings with microwave cooking are so precise there is likely to be less of a loss of nutrients during cooking.

Less Food Shrinkage
Cooked according to recipe instructions, there tends to be less shrinkage of foods because of the shorter cooking times needed.

Flexibility
Do not think of your microwave as a replacement for your conventional cooker but more of an adjunct or extra. Use it with your conventional cooker for greater flexibility and convenience in preparing meals. For example, shorten the cooking time of a slow-cooking casserole by pre-cooking in the microwave and finishing in the conventional oven. That way you will have a delicious meal in a shorter time with all the flavours and tenderness only associated with conventional cooking.

Foods That Do not Cook Well in the Microwave

Eggs in Shells
These are liable to explode due to the intense heat and pressure that builds up within the shell. Only cook eggs when they have been removed from their shells as in poaching, frying, scrambling and baking.

Pancakes
These reheat well but they will not crisp. For crispy results, place the pancakes under a preheated hot grill just before serving.

Popcorn
This is too dry to attract microwave energy.

Yorkshire Puddings and Soufflés
These rise beautifully then fall flat – the quick cooking times do not allow the mixtures to set to a rigid structure.

Meringues
Meringues tend to explode and will not dry out with microwave cooking.

Liquids in Bottles

Check that any bottles do not have too narrow necks when using in the microwave. The pressure that builds up with speedy heating can cause the bottle to shatter.

Very Large Food Loads

The microwave will cope with large food loads but the time advantage over conventional cooking may quickly be eroded. Calculate the cooking time beforehand for comparison.

Deep Fat Frying

This is generally not recommended in the microwave since deep fat frying requires prolonged high heating and can cause burns.

Menu Planning with the Microwave

It often takes a long time to learn the skills of planning and preparing a balanced meal. Choose different courses for a meal that offer variety, colour and moreover balanced nutrients. Cook foods also according to their characteristics.

Cook those foods first that will require some standing time. Other last minute foods can be cooked during this standing time. Other dishes that can be prepared in advance can be quickly reheated at the last possible moment and still taste freshly-cooked.

As a general rule, start cooking the main or meat dish first. Meats, fish and poultry cooked in a sauce or gravy will generally improve in flavour if left to stand for a little while before serving.

Make starters and desserts well ahead wherever possible and reheat where appropriate. Bread rolls and last minute accompaniments can literally be reheated while guests are preparing to sit down!

Having food ready at the right time is quite an art — with the microwave you have a friend — and if you go a little wrong it will often help you out. If food becomes too cold then simply reheat it for a few minutes: no one will ever know.

Suggested Menus

3 Course Formal Lunch for 4

Potted shrimps (see page 41)
Lamb kebabs (see page 66)
Green salad
Golden pudding (see page 160)

Buffet Lunch for 4

Farmhouse pâté (see page 36)
Smoked haddock and egg flan
(see page 60) *or* Redcurrant stuffed lamb
(cold, see page 66)
Corn coleslaw with peanut dressing
(see page 141)
Crunchy blackcurrant cheesecake
(see page 157)
Horkey punch (see page 187)

Informal Supper for 4

Chilli corn carne (see page 82)
Jacket potatoes (see page 133)
or Herby sausage lasagne (see page 117)
Green salad
Strawberry and pistachio refrigerator cake
(see page 173)
Mulled ale (see page 187)

Celebration Dinner for 4

Minestrone (see page 38)
Citrus leg of lamb (see page 69)
Bean and bacon savoury (see page 136)
Boiled new potatoes (see page 133)
Strawberry and tangerine mousses
(see page 157)
Gaelic coffee (see page 185)

Cleaning the Microwave Oven

Since the walls, base and ceiling of a microwave oven stay comparatively cool during cooking the microwave is a very easy piece of equipment to keep clean. Food will not burn or char onto the surfaces and any spatterings can simply be wiped away with a damp cloth, they will not bake on. Wipe up any spills as they occur however, since if you do not they will continue to absorb microwave energy leaving less to cook the food itself.

Both the exterior and the interior of the oven can be wiped with a soapy cloth, although make sure you do not allow water to drip through the vents into the electrical workings of the oven. Some manufacturers supply a special microwave cleaning agent which also deodorises the oven cavity. To make your own cleaning and deodorising agent, place a bowl containing 3 parts water to 1 part lemon juice in the oven cavity and cook on *Full Power* for 5–10 minutes. Wipe the surfaces dry with a clean cloth.

Any removable shelves, bases or removable turntables should also be washed regularly in warm soapy water and door seals should be washed, cleaned and checked regularly for a good seal and fit.

If your microwave also has a disposable and removable filter remember to clean, replace or service the filter according to the specific manufacturer's instructions.

Siting the Microwave Oven

All that you require to site and install a portable microwave oven is a firm surface and a suitable fused power socket outlet to match the plug. A kitchen work surface, a table in the dining area or other suitable surface are all recommended. Make sure that you do not cover any venting and that there is sufficient space near the venting for the free circulation of air. It is of course possible to move the microwave around and site it according to your needs at any one time. Use the microwave in the kitchen, dining room, outside for parties and barbecues or even take away with you to holiday homes and caravans for maximum use.

Many kitchen and appliance manufacturers also now make fitting kits and housing units so that you can build-in the microwave with your other domestic appliances for a totally integrated look. Such kits and housing units will take into account the venting space required for such building-in.

Safety

All microwave ovens for sale on the British and American market have had to undergo rigorous checks for safety and are controlled by legislation to ensure they are safe. These controls only refer to the oven before it is sold. To ensure that your oven is in good working and safe order it is recommended that you have your microwave checked by a reputable dealer or service network every 12 months, or as recommended by the manufacturer.

Those controls aside, the microwave is one of the safest electrical and cooking appliances around in the home today. It does not get hot so there is little risk of burning, it is heavy enough to be stable in most situations so is not liable to be knocked over like a saucepan and can be easily sited out of reach of young inquisitive hands.

Before You Start To Cook

Microwave cooking is very different from conventional cooking and it is for this reason that I strongly recommend you read the introductory know-how section to this book.

The recipes that follow have all been tested on a 700 watt microwave oven with variable control, perhaps the most popular domestic microwave oven. If your microwave oven has a higher power wattage, reduce the cooking times slightly. If your microwave oven has a lower power wattage, then increase the cooking times slightly.

Most recipes refer to cooking on *Full Power* (that is, working at maximum cooking speed or 100% input). Variable power settings refer to the oven working at the following power inputs:

Full Power	=	100% input
Medium/High Power	=	80% input
Medium Power	=	60% input
Defrost Power	=	40% input
Low Power	=	20% input

The manufacturer's instruction booklet, accompanying your microwave oven, will tell you the appropriate guide, either numerical or descriptive, that corresponds with these inputs if the description above is not applicable to your make of oven.

Metric measurements may vary from one recipe to another within this book. It is essential to follow *either* metric, Imperial or American measures. The recipes have been specially balanced to get the very best results whether using metric, Imperial or American measures so it is important not to interchange quantities.

Soups, Starters and Snacks

Most busy hostesses realise how useful it is to have a made-ahead cold starter on ice for a meal. Many more microwave hostesses are also now appreciating just how useful it is to serve piping hot soups and starters with the minimum of fuss – the microwave will take care of any last minute reheating or cooking, and while you are enjoying yourself with the guests.

Last minute luxury accompaniments like warm bread rolls will also become an everyday possibility with the help of the microwave.

The microwave will of course still help to make all those delicious cold starters like pâtés, mousses and potted shellfish – and in very little time, but where it is an extra bonus is in making tasty home-made soups in a fraction of the time it normally takes.

Piles of washing up will also become a thing of the past if you cook, reheat and serve in the same dish. It also means there is little fear of foods becoming too cold before guests are seated – and if they do, then simply reheat in the microwave for a couple of minutes for piping hot freshness.

Farmhouse pâté

Power setting Medium
Total cooking time 8 minutes

225 g/8 oz streaky bacon (U.S. ½ lb bacon slices), rinds removed
225 g/8 oz pig's liver, minced (U.S. ½ lb ground pork liver)
225 g/8 oz pork shoulder, minced (U.S. ½ lb ground pork)
225 g/8 oz (U.S. 1 cup) pork sausagemeat
1 small onion, peeled and finely chopped
1 clove garlic, crushed
½ teaspoon dried mixed herbs
salt and freshly ground black pepper

Line a 450-g/1-lb terrine with the bacon. Mix the liver with the pork, sausagemeat, onion, garlic, herbs and seasoning to taste. Spoon the mixture into the lined terrine, packing down well. Cover with absorbent kitchen towel and cook for 3 minutes. Allow to stand for 5 minutes.

Cook the pâté for a further 3 minutes. Give the terrine a half turn and cook for a further 2 minutes. Remove and cover with foil. Press down and weight until cold. Chill for 2–4 hours.

To serve, unmould onto a serving dish and cut in slices. Serve with crusty bread and a little salad. **Serves 6–8**

Tomato soup

(Illustrated on title spread)

Power setting Full
Total cooking time 22–24 minutes

50 g/2 oz (U.S. ¼ cup) butter
2 onions, peeled and chopped
50 g/2 oz (U.S. ½ cup) flour
900 ml/1½ pints hot chicken stock (U.S. 3¾ cups hot chicken bouillon)
900 g/2 lb tomatoes, peeled, seeds removed and chopped
2 tablespoons tomato purée (U.S. 3 tablespoons tomato paste)
1 teaspoon Worcestershire sauce
1 teaspoon dried basil
½ teaspoon sugar
salt and freshly ground black pepper
150 ml/¼ pint double cream (U.S. ⅔ cup heavy cream)
chopped parsley to garnish

Place the butter and onion in a bowl and cook for 4 minutes. Add the flour, mixing well and cook for 1 minute. Gradually add the stock and cook for 4 minutes, stirring every 1 minute to make a thick smooth sauce. Add the tomatoes, tomato purée, Worcestershire sauce, basil, sugar and seasoning to taste. Cover with cling film, snipping two holes in the top for the steam to escape. Cook for 10–12 minutes. Purée in a blender until smooth.

Cook for a further 2 minutes. Stir in the cream and cook for 1 minute. Serve garnished with chopped parsley. **Serves 4–6**

Potted bacon

(Illustrated on pages 34–35)

Power setting Full
Total cooking time 2 minutes

100 g/4 oz (U.S. ½ cup) butter
350 g/12 oz lean cooked hock or collar bacon, minced
(U.S. ¾ lb ground cooked smoked hock)
4 tablespoons double cream (U.S. ⅓ cup heavy cream)
1 tablespoon chopped parsley
1 teaspoon made mustard
2 tablespoons (U.S. 3 tablespoons) dry sherry
pinch of ground nutmeg
freshly ground black pepper
bay leaves to garnish

Place the butter in a bowl and cook for 2 minutes to melt. Mix half of the melted butter with the bacon, cream, parsley, mustard, sherry, nutmeg and black pepper to taste. Pack into one large or six small terrines. Pour the remaining melted butter over the top to coat. Chill to set.

Garnish the potted bacon with bay leaves and serve with warm crusty bread. **Serves 6**

Minestrone soup

Power setting Full
Total cooking time 26 minutes

3 tablespoons (U.S. $\frac{1}{4}$ cup) oil
1 clove garlic, crushed
1 onion, peeled and sliced
2 stalks celery, chopped
1 large carrot, peeled and chopped
4 rashers streaky bacon (U.S. 4 bacon slices), finely chopped
225 g/8 oz (U.S. 3 cups) cabbage, finely chopped
4 teaspoons tomato purée (U.S. 4 teaspoons tomato paste)
900 ml/1$\frac{1}{2}$ pints beef stock (U.S. 3$\frac{3}{4}$ cups beef bouillon)
1 tablespoon chopped parsley
salt and freshly ground black pepper
1 (425-g/15-oz) can red kidney beans
grated Parmesan cheese to serve

Place the oil in a large bowl and cook for 1 minute. Add the garlic, onion, celery, carrot and bacon and cook for 6 minutes. Add the cabbage, tomato purée, stock, parsley and seasoning to taste. Cook for 10 minutes, stirring halfway through the cooking time.

Add the beans and their can juice, mixing well. Cook for a further 9 minutes. Serve sprinkled with Parmesan cheese. **Serves 6**

Dutch vermicelli soup

Power setting Full and Medium
Total cooking time 24–26 minutes

Soup
25 g/1 oz (U.S. 2 tablespoons) butter
1 onion, peeled and chopped
25 g/1 oz (U.S. $\frac{1}{4}$ cup) flour
1.75 litres/3 pints chicken stock (U.S. 3$\frac{3}{4}$ pints chicken bouillon)
1 teaspoon ground mace
salt and freshly ground black pepper
50 g/2 oz (U.S. $\frac{1}{2}$ cup) fine vermicelli pasta
2 tablespoons chopped parsley
Meatballs
225 g/8 oz minced beef (U.S. $\frac{1}{2}$ lb ground beef)
75 g/3 oz (U.S. $\frac{3}{4}$ cup) Edam cheese, grated
1 egg, beaten
$\frac{1}{4}$ teaspoon ground nutmeg

Place the butter in a large bowl and cook on *Full Power* for 1 minute to melt. Add the onion and cook on *Full Power* for 2 minutes. Stir in the flour, mixing well to blend. Stir in the stock, mace and seasoning to taste. Cover and cook on *Full Power* for 6–8 minutes until thickened.

Meanwhile for the meatballs, mix the beef with the cheese, egg and nutmeg. Roll into small balls. Add the meatballs to the soup with the vermicelli. Cover and cook on *Medium Power* for 15 minutes, stirring halfway through the cooking time. Stir in parsley. **Serves 6**

Hearty leek and pasta soup

Power setting Full
Total cooking time 32 minutes

900 g/2 lb leeks, sliced
1 onion, peeled and chopped
25 g/1 oz (U.S. 2 tablespoons) butter
1 large potato, peeled and sliced
1 litre/1¾ pints hot chicken stock (U.S. 4¼ cups hot
chicken bouillon)
175 g/6 oz (U.S. 1½ cups) soup pasta, i.e. alphabet,
stars or shells
salt and freshly ground black pepper

Place the leeks, onion and butter in a large bowl. Cover and cook for 8 minutes. Add the potato, cover and cook for 8 minutes. Add the stock, cover and cook for 6 minutes. Purée in a blender until smooth.

Add the soup pasta and seasoning to taste. Cover and cook for 10 minutes. Allow to stand for 5–10 minutes before serving. **Serves 4–6**

Dutch bean soup

Power setting Full and Medium
Total cooking time 19 minutes

25 g/1 oz (U.S. 2 tablespoons) butter
1 onion, peeled and finely chopped
15 g/½ oz plain flour (U.S. 2 tablespoons all-purpose
flour)
1 (425-g/15-oz) can red kidney beans
1.15 litres/2 pints (U.S. 5 cups) water
1 teaspoon salt
¼ teaspoon paprika pepper
¼ teaspoon ground nutmeg
1 bay leaf
1 tablespoon chopped parsley

Place the butter in a large bowl and cook on *Full Power* for 1 minute to melt. Add the onion, cover and cook on *Full Power* for 2 minutes. Add the flour and mix well. Gradually add the beans and their can juice, blending well. Stir in the water, salt, paprika, nutmeg and bay leaf. Cover and cook on *Full Power* for 8 minutes. Stir well to mix.

Cover and cook on *Medium Power* for 8 minutes. Remove and discard the bay leaf. Stir in the parsley and serve hot with toast fingers if liked. **Serves 4**

Chilled cucumber and cheese soup

Power setting Full
Total cooking time 2½ minutes

1 tablespoon oil
1 small onion, chopped
225 g/8 oz (U.S. 2 cups) Gouda cheese, grated
2 cucumbers, coarsely chopped
2 tablespoons (U.S. 3 tablespoons) lemon juice
1 tablespoon dried mixed herbs
300 ml/½ pint chicken stock (U.S. 1¼ cups chicken bouillon)
salt and freshly ground black pepper

Place the oil and onion in a small bowl. Cover and cook for 2½ minutes. Purée in a blender with the cheese, cucumber, lemon juice, mixed herbs, chicken stock and seasoning to taste until well mixed. Chill thoroughly before serving. **Serves 6**

Variations
Chilled cucumber, chive and Edam soup Prepare and cook as above but use 225 g/8 oz (U.S. 2 cups) grated Edam cheese instead of the Gouda. Sprinkle with snipped chives before serving.

Chilled celery, cucumber and cheese soup Prepare and cook as above but use 225 g/8 oz (U.S. 2 cups) chopped celery instead of one of the cucumbers. Place the celery in a bowl, cover and cook for 4 minutes then allow to cool before using as above. **Total cooking time 6½ minutes**

Chilled cucumber, watercress and cheese soup Prepare and cook as above but use the trimmed leaves of 1 bunch of watercress instead of one of the cucumbers.

Spring onion, cucumber and cheese soup Prepare and cook as above but use 6 chopped spring onions (U.S. 6 chopped scallions) instead of the onion.

Potted shrimps

Power setting Full
Total cooking time 2½ minutes

175 g/6 oz (U.S. ¾ cup) butter, diced
350 g/12 oz peeled shrimps (U.S. 2 cups shelled
shrimp)
salt
cayenne pepper
Garnish
parsley sprigs
lemon wedges

Place the butter in a bowl and cook for 2½ minutes to melt. Add the shrimps, salt and cayenne to taste. Divide evenly between four small ramekin dishes and chill to set.

Garnish with parsley sprigs and lemon wedges and serve with toast. **Serves 4**

Variations
Potted shrimps with capers Prepare and cook as above but add 2 tablespoons (U.S. 3 tablespoons) chopped capers to the shrimps, mixing well.
Potted sherried shrimps Prepare and cook as above but marinate the shrimps in 1–2 tablespoons (U.S. 1–3 tablespoons) dry sherry before mixing with the butter and seasonings.
Potted crab Prepare and cook as above but use 350 g/12 oz (U.S. ¾ lb) flaked crabmeat instead of shrimps.
Potted smoked oysters and shrimps Prepare and cook as above but use 250 g/9 oz peeled shrimps (U.S. 1½ cups shelled shrimp) with a drained 105-g/3⅔-oz can smoked oysters.
Potted shrimps with anchovies Prepare and cook as above but add 4 chopped anchovies to the shrimps before mixing with the butter and seasonings.
Potted mixed seafood Prepare and cook as above but use 350 g/12 oz (U.S. ¾ lb) mixed cooked seafood instead of just shrimps. Ideal mixtures include shrimps, crabmeat, oysters, mussels, flaked sardine, flaked lobster and anchovy fillets.

Queen Juliana's salmon mousse

Power setting Full
Total cooking time 4–6 minutes

40 g/1½ oz powdered gelatine (u.s. 6 envelopes
gelatin)
450 ml/¾ pint chicken stock (u.s. 2 cups chicken
bouillon)
3 (212-g/7½-oz) cans red salmon, drained
4 teaspoons tomato purée (u.s. 4 teaspoons tomato
paste)
250 g/9 oz (u.s. 1 cup plus 2 tablespoons) butter
250 g/9 oz (u.s. 2¼ cups) Gouda cheese, grated
freshly ground black pepper
Garnish
cucumber slices
mustard and cress
unpeeled prawns (u.s. unshelled shrimp)

Soak the gelatine in the stock in a jug to soften for 2
minutes. Cook for 1–2 minutes until the gelatine had
dissolved.

Remove any skin and bones from the salmon and
mix with the tomato purée. Place the butter in a bowl
and cook for 3–4 minutes to melt. Place the gelatine
mixture, salmon mixture, butter, cheese and pepper to
taste in a blender and purée until smooth. Pour into a
greased 20-cm/8-inch spring form mould and chill to
set.

Unmould by dipping the mould briefly into hot
water and inverting onto a plate.

Garnish with cucumber slices, mustard and cress and
whole prawns. Serve with slices of brown bread and
butter if liked. **Serves 8–10**

Variations
Queen Juliana's salmon and tuna mousse Prepare
and cook as above but use a drained 212-g/7½-oz can
tuna instead of one of the cans of salmon.
Queen Juliana's salmon and prawn mousse Prepare and cook as above but use two drained 92-g/3¼-oz
cans peeled prawns instead of one of the cans of salmon.
Queen Juliana's salmon and crab mousse Prepare
and cook as above but use a drained 198-g/7-oz can
crabmeat instead of one of the cans of salmon.

Smoked haddock mousse

Power setting Full
Total cooking time 5½–6 minutes

225 g/8 oz (U.S. ½ lb) smoked haddock fillet
15 g/½ oz powdered gelatine (U.S. 2 envelopes gelatin)
150 ml/¼ pint chicken stock (U.S. ⅔ cup chicken bouillon)
1½ tablespoons (U.S. 2 tablespoons) lemon juice
75 g/3 oz (U.S. ¾ cup) Gouda cheese, grated
freshly ground black pepper
75 g/3 oz (U.S. 6 tablespoons) butter
1 tablespoon chopped parsley
Garnish
lemon wedges
cucumber slices
parsley sprigs
cress

Place the haddock in a dish with 1 tablespoon water. Cover and cook for 3–3½ minutes until cooked. Skin and flake and place in a blender.

Soak the gelatine in the chicken stock in a small bowl to soften for 2 minutes. Cook for 1 minute until the gelatine has dissolved. Allow to cool slightly then pour into the blender. Add the lemon juice, cheese and pepper to taste. Blend until smooth.

Place the butter in a bowl and cook for 1½ minutes to melt. Stir into the haddock mixture with the parsley. Pour into a medium-sized loaf tin and chill until set.

To serve, dip the tin briefly in hot water. Unmould the mousse onto a serving plate. Slice and garnish with lemon wedges, cucumber slices, parsley sprigs and cress. Serve with toast or crisp crackers and a little salad.
Serves 6

Variations
Smoked trout mousse Prepare and cook as above but use 225 g/8 oz (U.S. ½ lb) cooked smoked flaked trout instead of the smoked haddock fillet. There is no need to cook the fish prior to blending with the remaining ingredients. **Total cooking time 2½ minutes**
Savoury kipper mousse Prepare and cook as above but use 1 (212-g/7½-oz) packet frozen kipper fillets instead of the smoked haddock fillet. Cook from frozen as above for 5 minutes. **Total cooking time 7½ minutes**

Crispy sweetcorn and liver starter kebabs

Power setting Full
Total cooking time 21–23 minutes

3 tablespoons (U.S. ¼ cup) oil
350 g/12 oz lamb's liver (U.S. ¾ lb lamb liver), cut
into squares
4 lean rashers back bacon (U.S. 4 Canadian bacon
slices), rinds removed
50 g/2 oz (U.S. ½ cup) button mushrooms
4 frozen corn on the cobs, thawed
2 teaspoons lemon juice
salt and freshly ground black pepper
3 wholewheat and bran light crispbreads, crushed

Place the oil in a deep dish and cook for 1 minute. Add the liver and cook for 3 minutes, stirring halfway through the cooking time. Remove with a slotted spoon and set aside.

Make the bacon rashers into small rolls and secure with wooden cocktail sticks. Place in the bowl and cook for 3 minutes. Remove with a slotted spoon and set aside. Add the mushrooms to the cooking juices, toss well to coat and cook for 2 minutes. Remove with a slotted spoon.

Cut each corn on the cob into six thin slices. Thread the liver, mushrooms, bacon and corn alternately onto four wooden skewers. Add the lemon juice with seasoning to taste to the cooking juices. Brush the kebabs liberally with this mixture. Cook for 4 minutes.

Roll the kebabs in the crispbread crumbs and cook for a further 8–10 minutes until cooked. Serve on a bed of rice mixed with cooked peas if liked.
Note: Metal skewers may be used in the microwave if the food is packed well together on the skewers, leaving very little metal exposed. **Serves 4**

Spicy bean pâté

Power setting Full
Total cooking time 4 minutes

1 (425-g/15-oz) can red kidney beans
1 clove garlic, crushed
1 tablespoon tomato purée (U.S. 1 tablespoon tomato
paste)
1 teaspoon Worcestershire sauce
1 teaspoon lemon juice
few drops Tabasco sauce (U.S. few drops hot pepper
sauce)
salt and freshly ground black pepper
parsley sprigs to garnish
crispbreads to serve

Drain the beans and place in a bowl. Add 3 tablespoons (U.S. ¼ cup) of the can juice with the garlic, tomato purée, Worcestershire sauce, lemon juice, Tabasco sauce and seasoning to taste. Cover and cook for 4 minutes, stirring halfway through the cooking time.

Place in a blender and purée until smooth. Spoon into four individual dishes and chill. Garnish with parsley sprigs and serve with crispbreads. **Serves 4**

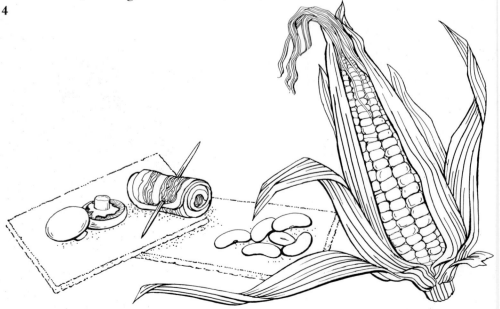

Stuffed smoked salmon rolls

Power setting Full
Total cooking time 4–4½ minutes

20 g/¾ oz (U.S. 1½ tablespoons) butter
20 g/¾ oz (U.S. 3 tablespoons) flour
150 ml/¼ pint fish or light chicken stock (U.S. ⅔ cup fish or light chicken bouillon)
150 ml/¼ pint (U.S. ⅔ cup) rosé wine
100 g/4 oz (U.S. 1 cup) Edam cheese, finely grated
3 eggs, separated
1 tablespoon lemon juice
salt and freshly ground black pepper
20 g/¾ oz powdered gelatine (U.S. 3 envelopes gelatin)
150 ml/¼ pint double cream (U.S. ⅔ cup heavy cream), lightly whipped
50 g/2 oz peeled prawns (U.S. ⅓ cup shelled shrimp)
12 slices smoked salmon
Garnish
whole prawns
lemon slices
parsley sprigs

Place the butter in a bowl and cook for ½ minute to melt. Add the flour and mix well. Gradually add the stock and wine, a little at a time. Cook for 3–3½ minutes, stirring every 1 minute until the sauce is smooth and thickened. Stir in the cheese. Add the egg yolks, lemon juice and seasoning to taste, mixing well.

Soak the gelatine in 3 tablespoons water in a small bowl to soften for 2 minutes. Cook for about ½ minute until the gelatine has dissolved. Stir into the sauce.

Cool the sauce until it reaches setting point then fold in the cream. Whisk the egg whites until they stand in stiff peaks and fold into the sauce mixture with the prawns. Chill to set.

Place some cheese and prawn soufflé mixture in the centre of each slice of smoked salmon and roll up. Serve garnished with whole prawns, lemon slices and parsley sprigs. **Serves 6**

Variations
Stuffed smoked salmon and crab rolls Prepare and cook as above but use a drained and flaked 92-g/3¼-oz can crabmeat instead of the prawns.
Stuffed smoked salmon and caviar rolls Prepare and cook as above but place 1 teaspoon caviar or mock caviar on top of the cheese mixture on each smoked salmon roll before rolling up.

Continental loaf

Power setting Full
Total cooking time 2–3 minutes

1 large crusty loaf
50 g/2 oz (U.S. $\frac{1}{4}$ cup) butter
8 slices cooked continental-style ham
8 slices quick-melting cheese

Make eight cuts equally across the length of the loaf almost to the base. Spread thinly between the slices with butter. Place one slice of ham and one slice of cheese in each cut. Cover loosely with greaseproof paper. Cook for 2–3 minutes until the cheese melts.

Cut between the bread slices to serve as a substantial snack. **Serves 4**

Variations

Continental rolls Prepare and cook as above but divide the ham and cheese between four crusty rolls. Make two vertical cuts into the rolls to spread the butter and to hold the cheese and ham. Re-arrange the rolls halfway through the cooking time to ensure even heating.

Continental garlic loaf Prepare and cook as above but mix the butter with 1–2 crushed cloves garlic before spreading on the loaf.

Continental herb loaf Prepare and cook as above but mix the butter with 1 teaspoon mixed dried herbs or 2 teaspoons chopped fresh herbs before spreading on the loaf.

Continental tomato loaf Prepare and cook as above but mix the butter with 2 teaspoons tomato purée (U.S. 2 teaspoons tomato paste) before spreading on the loaf. Place slices of tomato with the ham in the loaf if liked and cook for $2\frac{1}{2}$–$3\frac{1}{2}$ minutes. **Total cooking time $2\frac{1}{2}$–$3\frac{1}{2}$ minutes**

Continental fish loaf Prepare and cook as above but mix the butter with 1 teaspoon anchovy essence if liked before spreading on the loaf. Use 225 g/8 oz (U.S. $\frac{1}{2}$ lb) sliced smoked fish or flaked fish instead of the continental ham.

Beef and horseradish loaf Prepare and cook as above but mix the butter with 2 teaspoons horseradish relish before spreading on the loaf. Fill the loaf with 16 slices cooked beef and omit the cheese and ham.

Continental sausage loaf Prepare and cook as above but mix the butter with 1–2 teaspoons made mustard before spreading on the loaf. Use 8 slices cooked continental sausage instead of the continental ham.

Beanfeast snack

Power setting Full
Total cooking time 2–2¼ minutes

15 g/½ oz (U.S. 1 tablespoon) butter
1 egg, beaten
1 tablespoon milk
4 tablespoons (U.S. ⅓ cup) baked beans
2 bran and rye crispbreads
2 slices tomato
parsley sprig to garnish

Place half of the butter in a bowl. Beat the egg with the milk. Add to the bowl and cook for 1–1¼ minutes, stirring halfway through the cooking time.

Place the beans in another bowl, cover and cook for 1 minute. Spread the crispbreads with the remaining butter. Place on a plate. Spoon the scrambled egg around the edge of the crispbreads. Spoon the beans into the centre of the egg nest. Top with the tomato slices and garnish with the parsley sprig. Serve at once.
Serves 1

Fruit topper snack

Power setting Full
Total cooking time 12–14 minutes

450 g/1 lb mixed dried fruits
450 ml/¾ pint (U.S. 2 cups) cold water
4 tablespoons (U.S. ⅓ cup) clear honey
1 cinnamon stick
3–4 cloves
¼ teaspoon ground allspice
strip of lemon rind
150 ml/¼ pint (U.S. ⅔ cup) thick set natural yogurt
4 crispbreads, coarsely crushed
4 teaspoons toasted muesli

Place the fruits, cold water, honey, cinnamon, cloves, allspice and lemon rind in a large deep dish, cover and leave to stand for 2 hours.

Cover loosely with cling film and cook for 12–14 minutes or until the fruit is tender, giving the dish an occasional shake during cooking. Remove the cinnamon stick, cloves and lemon rind. Serve hot or chilled, topped with a little yogurt, crushed crispbreads and muesli. **Serves 4**

Guide to heating coffee, tea and milk

For most people, a quick snack implies a quick cup of coffee or tea and a biscuit. The microwave oven will cope with this task effortlessly. Follow the guidelines below for piping hot results, remembering too that if the tea or coffee becomes too cold to drink then simply reheat it quickly in the microwave.

Black coffee

	Time in mins on Full Power
600 ml/1 pint (U.S. 2½ cups)	4½–5
1.2 litres/2 pints (U.S. 5 cups)	7–7½

Milk

150 ml/¼ pint (U.S. ⅔ cup)	1–1½
300 ml/½ pint (U.S. 1¼ cups)	2–2½

Coffee and milk together

600 ml/1 pint (U.S. 2½ cups) cold coffee and 150 ml/¼ pint (U.S. ⅔ cup) cold milk.	5–5½
1.2 litres/2 pints (U.S. 5 cups) cold coffee and 300 ml/½ pint (U.S. 1¼ cups) cold milk	8–8½

Tea

Follow the guidelines for black coffee above using water only. Add the tea leaves or tea bags at the end of the heating time and leave until the desired strength of tea is obtained. Remove and discard the bags if liked or strain and serve.

Fish and Seafood

Can you believe it – a piece of fish cooked in just 2–3 minutes? It is not only believable but possible with the microwave oven. Whole fish, fish fillets, fish steaks and cutlets cooked in the very minimum of time to a firm but delicate texture.

The range of fish dishes that can be cooked in the microwave is enormous – fish in crumbs, in cream, in sauces or simply with just a knob of butter – the choice is yours.

Goodbye to lingering cooking smells too – the microwave with its fast speed of cooking keeps these very much at bay.

Remember to pierce the skin of large whole fish or large fish fillets before cooking so that steam can escape. Also line a dish with absorbent kitchen towel before cooking fish steaks like salmon or halibut – this will help to absorb the coagulated juices as they form on the skin during cooking. Protect too those sensitive areas of fish that are vulnerable to overcooking – the fish head and tail – with strips of foil for perfect results.

Guide to defrosting fish and shellfish

Fish or Shellfish	Quantity	Time in minutes on Defrost power
Crabmeat	450 g (1 lb)	14–16
Fish fillets	450 g (1 lb)	6–8
Fish steaks	1 (175-g/6-oz) steak	2–2$\frac{1}{2}$
	2 (175-g/6-oz) steaks	3–4$\frac{1}{2}$
Lobster – whole	450 g (1 lb)	12
	675 g (1$\frac{1}{2}$ lb)	16–18
Prawns, Scampi, Jumbo shrimp and Pacific prawns	450 g (1 lb)	8–9
Scallops	450 g (1 lb)	9–10
Shrimps	450 g (1 lb)	7–8$\frac{1}{2}$
Whole fish	1 (225–275-g/8–10-oz) whole fish	4–6
	2 (225–275-g/8–10-oz) whole fish	10–12
	1 (1.4-kg–1.8-kg/3–4-lb) whole fish	20–22

Note To defrost fish and shellfish on **Full power**, cook on high for $\frac{1}{4}$–$\frac{1}{2}$ minute, allow to stand for 2 minutes. Repeat until evenly thawed throughout, turning and rotating the food and dish occasionally.

Guide to cooking fish and shellfish

Fish or Shellfish	Quantity	Cooking time in minutes on Full power	Special points
Bass – whole	450 g (1 lb)	5–7	Shield the head and tail with foil. Cut the skin in 2–3 places to prevent the skin from bursting.
Cod – steaks	450 g (1 lb)	3–5	Cover with greaseproof paper before cooking.
– fillets	450 g (1 lb)	6–7	Place the fillet rolls to the centre of the dish or shield with foil. Cut the skin in 2–3 places to prevent the skin from bursting.
Haddock – steaks	450 g (1 lb)	3–5	Cover with greaseproof paper before cooking.
– fillets	450 g (1 lb)	5–7	Place the fillet tails to the centre of the dish or shield with foil. Cut the skin in 2–3 places to prevent the skin from bursting.
Halibut – steaks	450 g (1 lb)	4–5	Cover with greaseproof paper before cooking.
Kippers – whole	1	$1\frac{1}{2}$–2	Cover with cling film.
Lobster – whole	450 g (1 lb)	6–8	Allow to stand for 5 minutes before serving. Turn over halfway through the cooking time.
– tails	450 g (1 lb)	5–6	Turn tails over halfway through the cooking time.
Prawns, Scampi, Jumbo shrimp and Pacific prawns	450 g (1 lb)	5–6	Arrange prawns in a ring in a shallow dish and cover with cling film.
Red Snapper and Red mullet – whole	450 g (1 lb)	6–7	Shield the head and tail with foil. Cut the skin in 2–3 places to prevent the skin from bursting.
Salmon – steaks	450 g (1 lb)	3–5	Cover with greaseproof paper before cooking.
Salmon trout – whole	450 g (1 lb)	7–8	Shield the head and tail with foil. Cut the skin in 2–3 places to prevent the skin from bursting.
Scallops	450 g (1 lb)	5–7	Cover with dampened absorbent kitchen towel.
Shrimps	450 g (1 lb)	5–6	Arrange shrimps in a ring in a shallow dish and cover with cling film.
Smoked haddock – whole	450 g (1 lb)	4–6	Cover with cling film.
Trout – whole	450 g (1 lb)	7–9	Shield the head and tail with foil. Cut the skin in 2–3 places to prevent the skin from bursting.

Haddock roly poly

Power setting Full
Total cooking time 15 minutes

Suet pastry
225 g/8 oz self-raising flour (u.s. 2 cups all-purpose
flour sifted with 2 teaspoons baking powder)
sifted with a pinch of salt
100 g/4 oz (u.s. generous $\frac{3}{4}$ cup) shredded suet
150 ml/$\frac{1}{4}$ pint (u.s. $\frac{2}{3}$ cup) cold water
Filling
225 g/8 oz (u.s. $\frac{1}{2}$ lb) smoked haddock fillet
1 tablespoon oil
1 small onion, peeled and chopped
50 g/2 oz (u.s. $\frac{1}{2}$ cup) mushrooms, sliced
1 tablespoon capers
1 tablespoon chopped parsley
salt and freshly ground black pepper

Add the suet to the flour and mix well to blend. Add the
cold water and mix to a firm dough. Roll out to a 23-
cm/9-inch square.

Place the haddock in a dish with 3 tablespoons (u.s. $\frac{1}{4}$
cup) of water. Cook, covered for 3 minutes. Drain and
flake. Place the oil in a dish with the onion. Cover and
cook for 2 minutes. Add the mushrooms and cook for a
further 2 minutes. Add the fish, capers, parsley and
seasoning to taste. Spread over the pastry evenly, leaving
a 1-cm/$\frac{1}{2}$-inch border. Roll up and place seam-side down
on a piece of greaseproof paper and roll up loosely. Tie
the ends of the paper with string. Cover with cling film.
Cook for 8 minutes. Slice, garnish with chopped parsley
and serve with tomato sauce. **Serves 6**

Cheesy fish parcels

Power setting Full
Total cooking time 13–14 minutes

4 (175-g/6-oz) haddock or cod cutlets
Topping
2 tablespoons (u.s. 3 tablespoons) oil
1 onion, peeled and sliced
2 green peppers, seeds removed and sliced
4 tomatoes, peeled and finely sliced
100 g/4 oz (u.s. 1 cup) mushrooms, sliced
50 g/2 oz black olives, stoned (u.s. $\frac{1}{3}$ cup ripe olives,
pitted)
2 tablespoons (u.s. 3 tablespoons) lemon juice
$\frac{1}{2}$ teaspoon chopped fresh mixed herbs
salt and freshly ground black pepper
100 g/4 oz (u.s. 1 cup) Edam cheese, grated

Place the fish in a greased large shallow dish. Cover and
cook for 6–7 minutes, giving the dish a half turn
halfway through the cooking time. Leave to stand while
preparing the topping.

Place the oil in a bowl. Add the onion, peppers,
tomatoes and mushrooms. Cover and cook for 5
minutes, stirring halfway through the cooking time.
Add the olives, lemon juice, herbs and seasoning to
taste. Pile equal quantities of the vegetable mixture on
top of the fish cutlets. Sprinkle with the cheese and cook
for 2–3 minutes until the fish is hot and the cheese melts.

Brown under a preheated hot grill if liked. **Serves 4**

Cod with mustard and parsley sauce

Power setting Full
Total cooking time 11–12 minutes

75 g/3 oz (U.S. 6 tablespoons) butter
4 cod steaks
2 tablespoons (U.S. 3 tablespoons) seasoned flour
Sauce
40 g/1½ oz plain flour (U.S. 6 tablespoons all-purpose flour)
300 ml/½ pint (U.S. 1¼ cups) milk
1 tablespoon Dijon mustard
1 tablespoon chopped parsley
salt and freshly ground pepper

Preheat a large browning dish or skillet for 5 minutes (or according to the manufacturer's instructions). Add half the butter to the dish and swirl to coat. Dip the cod steaks in the flour and place on the dish. Cook for 3 minutes. Turn over and cook for a further 3½–4 minutes or until the fish is cooked and flakes easily. Cover with foil and leave to stand while preparing the sauce.

Place the remaining butter in a bowl and cook for 1 minute to melt. Stir in the flour. Gradually add the milk. Cook for 3½–4 minutes, stirring every 1 minute to make a smooth and thickened sauce. Stir in the mustard, parsley and seasoning to taste.

Transfer the fish to a heated serving plate and pour over the sauce. Garnish with lemon wedges. **Serves 4**

Marinated haddock with lemon

Power setting Full
Total cooking time 2 minutes

350 g/12 oz (U.S. ¾ lb) uncooked smoked haddock, skinned
2 tablespoons (U.S. 3 tablespoons) dried onions or 1 small onion, peeled and chopped
½ teaspoon dried mixed herbs
salt and freshly ground black pepper
grated rind and juice of 1 large lemon
2 tablespoons (U.S. 3 tablespoons) olive oil
Garnish
lemon twist
parsley sprigs

Cut the haddock into long thin strips and place in a bowl.

Place the onion in a bowl with the herbs, seasoning to taste, lemon rind and juice and oil. (If using dried onion, rehydrate first by soaking in 3 tablespoons (U.S. ¼ cup) water.) Cook for 2 minutes. Pour over the fish and toss well to coat. Cover and leave to marinate for at least 6 hours or overnight. Serve chilled. Garnish with a lemon twist and parsley sprigs and accompany with brown or rye bread. **Serves 4**

Fish and corn puffs

Power setting Full
Total cooking time 13 minutes

6 slices white bread, crusts removed
40 g/1½ oz (U.S. 3 tablespoons) butter
350 g/12 oz plaice fillets (U.S. ¾ lb flounder fillets),
skinned
salt and freshly ground black pepper
25 g/1 oz (U.S. ¼ cup) cheese, grated
2 eggs, beaten
3 tablespoons (U.S. ¼ cup) milk
1 (298-g/10½-oz) can cream style corn
1 teaspoon Worcestershire sauce

Lightly grease a medium-sized pie dish. Butter the bread slices and trim the plaice fillets to fit three of them. Place any fish trimmings on top and season to taste. Cover with the remaining bread slices, pressing them firmly together like sandwiches. Cut each 'sandwich' into four triangles and stand, points uppermost, in the dish. Sprinkle over the cheese.

Beat the eggs with the milk, corn and Worcestershire sauce. Carefully pour over the bread and cook, uncovered, for 3 minutes.

Press down the bread and fish triangles into the mixture and leave to stand for 5 minutes. Cook, uncovered, for a further 5 minutes, then leave to stand for 15 minutes. Cook, uncovered, for a further 5 minutes until hot and bubbly and firm to the touch. Place under a preheated hot grill until golden. Serve hot, garnished with parsley sprigs. **Serves 4**

Variations
Smoked fish and corn puffs Prepare and cook as above but use 350 g/12 oz (U.S. ¾ lb) smoked raw fish fillets instead of the plaice fillets. Smoked cod or haddock fillets if finely sliced make ideal choices.
Fish, corn and mushroom puffs Prepare and cook as above but sandwich the bread together with 50 g/2 oz (U.S. ½ cup) sliced mushrooms as well as the fish.

Stuffed mackerel

Power setting Full
Total cooking time 26–30 minutes

2 potatoes, peeled and chopped
2 carrots, peeled and chopped
150 ml/¼ pint (U.S. ⅔ cup) water
½ teaspoon salt
1 tablespoon made English mustard
1 onion, peeled and sliced into rings
4 small mackerel, cleaned
150 ml/¼ pint (U.S. ⅔ cup) dry white wine or cider

Place the potatoes and carrots in a dish with the water and salt. Cover and cook for 10–12 minutes until tender. Drain well and mix with the mustard and half of the onion rings. Stuff the centre of each fish with the potato mixture. Lay them side by side in a dish.

Pour over the wine or cider. Cut the skin in 2–3 places to prevent bursting. Cover with the remaining onion rings. Cover and cook for 16–18 minutes. Serve hot. **Serves 4**

Variations
Stuffed trout Prepare and cook as above but use 4 medium-sized gutted and cleaned trout instead of the small cleaned mackerel.

Stuffed celery and chive mackerel Prepare and cook as above but use 3 stalks chopped celery instead of the carrots and use chive mustard instead of English mustard if available. Alternatively mix 1 teaspoon snipped chives with the mustard.

Stuffed oaty mackerel Prepare and cook as above but only use 1 potato with the carrots. Cover and cook for 7–9 minutes, until tender. Drain well and mix with 25 g/1 oz (U.S. ⅓ cup) rolled oats, the mustard and half the onion rings. Continue as above. **Total cooking time 23–27 minutes**

Stuffed cod steaks in tomato sauce

Power setting Full
Total cooking time 13–17 minutes

50 g/2 oz (U.S. ¼ cup) butter
1 small onion, peeled and chopped
3 tablespoons (U.S. ¼ cup) fresh white breadcrumbs
1 (198-g/7-oz) can sweetcorn kernels, drained
1 tablespoon chopped parsley
100 g/4 oz (U.S. 1 cup) cheese, grated
salt and freshly ground black pepper
1 (376-g/13¼-oz) can tomato and onion cook-in-sauce
4 cod steaks

Place the butter in a bowl with the onion. Cover and cook for 3 minutes. Add the breadcrumbs, sweetcorn, parsley, cheese and seasoning to taste, mixing well.

Pour the cook-in-sauce into a shallow dish. Place the cod steaks on top. Divide the stuffing into four equal portions and pile on top of the cod steaks. Cook for 10–14 minutes until the fish is tender. Brown under a preheated hot grill if liked. **Serves 4**

Variations
Stuffed cod steaks in tomato and pepper sauce Prepare and cook as above but add 1 seeded and chopped green pepper to the cook-in-sauce.
Stuffed cod steaks in sweet and sour sauce Prepare and cook as above but use 1 (376-g/13¼-oz) can sweet and sour sauce instead of the tomato and onion sauce.
Stuffed cod steaks in white wine sauce Prepare and cook as above but use 1 (376-g/13¼-oz) can white wine sauce instead of the tomato and onion sauce.

West Country mussels

(Illustrated on pages 50–51)

Power setting Full
Total cooking time 11 minutes

1 tablespoon oil
1 small onion, peeled and chopped
1 clove garlic, crushed
1 tablespoon chopped parsley
1 tablespoon flour
300 ml/½ pint dry cider (U.S. 1¼ cups hard cider)
salt and freshly ground black pepper
2.25 litres/2 quarts (U.S. 5 pints) mussels, scrubbed

Place the oil, onion, garlic and parsley in a large bowl. Cook for 1 minute. Stir in the flour, mix well and gradually add the cider. Season to taste and cook for 2 minutes, stirring every ½ minute.

Add half of the mussels, tossing well to coat in the sauce. Cover and cook for 4 minutes, stirring halfway through the cooking time. Remove with a slotted spoon and place in a heated serving dish. (Discard any mussels that do not open.)

Add the remaining mussels and toss in the remaining sauce. Cover and cook for 4 minutes, stirring halfway through the cooking time. Add to the mussels already cooked in the serving dish. Serve at once. **Serves 2**

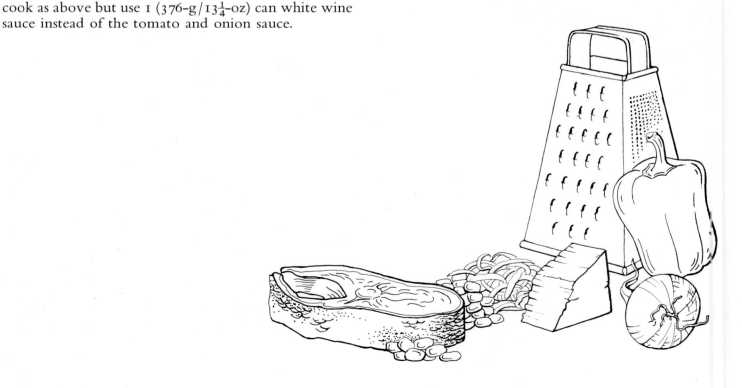

Smoked haddock and egg flan

(Illustrated on pages 50–51)

Power setting Full
Total cooking time 15½–17 minutes

Pastry
175 g/6 oz plain flour (U.S. 1½ cups all-purpose flour)
pinch of salt
75 g/3 oz (U.S. 6 tablespoons) butter
3 tablespoons (U.S. ¼ cup) water
Filling
2 (198-g/7-oz) packets frozen smoked haddock fillets
2 hard-boiled eggs (U.S. 2 hard-cooked eggs), chopped
¼ cucumber, chopped
6 tablespoons (U.S. ½ cup) mayonnaise
salt and freshly ground black pepper
¼ teaspoon paprika
15 g/½ oz powdered gelatine (U.S. 2 envelopes gelatin)
3 tablespoons water
cucumber and tomato slices to garnish

Sift the flour with the salt into a bowl. Rub in the butter until the mixture resembles fine breadcrumbs. Stir in the water and mix well to bind. Roll out on a lightly floured surface to a round large enough to line a 20-cm/8-inch flan dish. Press in firmly taking care not to stretch the pastry. Cut the pastry away leaving a 5 mm/¼ inch 'collar' above the dish (this allows for any shrinkage that may occur). Prick the base well with a fork. Line the inside, upright edge of the pastry case with a long strip of foil, about 4 cm/1½ inches wide. (This prevents the outer edges from overcooking.) Place a double thickness layer of absorbent kitchen towel over the base, easing into position around the edges to keep the foil in place. Cook for 4–4½ minutes, giving the dish a quarter turn every 1 minute. Remove the paper and foil and cook for a further 1–2 minutes. Allow to cool.

For the filling, place the frozen fish in a dish still in their plastic pouches or place in a dish and cover with cling film. Snip the pouch or cling film for the steam to escape. Cook for 10 minutes, giving the dish a half turn halfway through the cooking time. Drain and flake the fish. Allow to cool.

Mix the fish with the eggs, cucumber, mayonnaise, seasoning to taste and paprika. Soak the gelatine in the water in a small bowl to soften for 2 minutes. Cook for ½ minute until the gelatine has dissolved. Allow to cool slightly then stir into the fish mixture. Spoon into the cooked flan case and chill to set.

Garnish and cut into wedges to serve. **Serves 4–6**

Marinated salmon trout

(Illustrated on pages 50–51)

Power setting Full
Total cooking time 27 minutes

1 (1.8-kg/4-lb) salmon trout, cleaned
25 g/1 oz (U.S. 2 tablespoons) butter
1 small onion, peeled and chopped
2 teaspoons fresh tarragon or 1 teaspoon dried
grated rind of ½ lemon
salt and freshly ground black pepper
150 ml/¼ pint (U.S. ⅔ cup) dry white wine
Garnish
cucumber slices
lemon slices
mayonnaise

With a sharp knife, cut several deep slits along the length of the trout skin to allow steam to escape during cooking.

Place the butter in a bowl with the onion. Cover and cook for 3 minutes. Stir in the tarragon, lemon rind and seasoning to taste. Spoon this mixture into the body cavity of the fish. Place in a large shallow dish and pour over the wine. Cover and cook for 24 minutes, giving the dish a quarter turn every 6 minutes.

Allow to cool in the juices. Remove the skin from the salmon and discard. Serve the trout garnished with cucumber slices, lemon slices and mayonnaise. **Serves 6–8**

Poached salmon steaks

Power setting Full
Total cooking time 7 minutes

4 (175-g/6-oz) salmon steaks
2 tablespoons (U.S. 3 tablespoons) lemon juice
120 ml/4 fl oz (U.S. ½ cup) water
1 teaspoon salt

Place the salmon steaks in a shallow dish. Sprinkle with the lemon juice and leave to stand for 5 minutes.

Mix the water with the salt and pour over the salmon steaks. Cover and cook for 7 minutes, giving the dish a half turn every 2 minutes. Allow to stand for 5 minutes before serving.

Serve the salmon steaks hot with a Hollandaise sauce (see page 125) and vegetables in season, or serve cold with mayonnaise and salad. **Serves 4**

Meat, Poultry and Game

Cooking regular family meals can be quite a daunting task – especially if time or money are at a premium. The microwave will arm you with a wealth of ideas for quick, easy and nutritious meals for year round eating.

Those delicious steamed meat puddings, slow-cooking casseroles and hot-pots, once a luxury because of the time they took to prepare, can now come to the fore again for daily eating. Roast chicken, that wonderful standby, will also seem extra convenient when cooked in under 10 minutes per 450 g/1 lb.

However, it isn't just with mid-week eating that the microwave shows its expertise but also when cooking for special festive occasions. Large turkeys, game birds and meat roasts can be cooked in a fraction of the time they would take conventionally. Follow the tips in the section on browning (see page 18) if you plan to cook individual pieces of meat or a small roast that is unlikely to brown readily.

And if you're used to catering for a family with staggered meal times then you can be freed from the drudgery of the kitchen – simply reheat plated meals as each person arrives to just-cooked freshness.

Guide to defrosting meat

Meat	Defrosting time in minutes on Defrost power per 450 g (1 lb)	Guidelines
Beef – joints (*U.S. Roasts*)	9	Turn over at least once during the defrosting time.
– steaks (large)	8	Turn over at least once during the defrosting time.
– steaks (small)	4	Turn over at least once during the defrosting time.
– minced beef (*U.S. Ground beef*)	10	Break up with a fork during defrosting.
Lamb – joints (*U.S. Roasts*)	10	Turn over at least once during the defrosting time.
– chops	5	Turn over at least once during the defrosting time.
Pork – joints (*U.S. Roasts*)	$8\frac{1}{2}$	Turn over at least once during the defrosting time.
– chops	5	Turn over at least once during the defrosting time.
Veal – joints (*U.S. Roasts*)	9	Turn over at least once during the defrosting time.
Liver	4	Turn over at least once during the defrosting time.
Kidney	4	Turn over at least once during the defrosting time.

Note If your microwave does not have **Defrost power** then cook meat on **Full power** for 1 minute for every 450 g (1 lb). Allow to stand for 10 minutes. Repeat until the meat is thoroughly thawed.

Guide to cooking meat

Meat	Cooking time in minutes on Medium power per 450 g (1 lb)		Cooking time in minutes on Full power per 450 g (1 lb)	Guidelines
Beef				
Topside – rare	12		5–6	Choose a good quality joint with even fat covering and neat shape. Allow to stand for 15–20 minutes, wrapped in foil, before carving.
(*U.S. Beef* – medium	14		6–7	
round top) – well done	16		8–9	
Sirloin – rare	12		5–6	Choose a good quality joint with even fat covering and neat shape. Allow to stand for 15–20 minutes, wrapped in foil, before carving.
– medium	14		6–7	
– well done	16		8–9	
Rib – rare	12–13		$5\frac{1}{2}$–$6\frac{1}{2}$	Bone and roll ideally before cooking. Allow to stand for 15–30 minutes, wrapped in foil, before carving.
– medium	14–15		7–8	
– well done	16–17		8–10	
Minced beef (*U.S. Ground beef*)	14–16		10–12	
Rump steak – rare	—		2	Preheat the browning dish according to manufacturer's instructions. Add meat and brown. Turn over and cook for recommended time.
(*U.S. Top* – medium			2–4	
round steak) – well done			4	
Fillet steak – rare	—		2	Preheat the browning dish according to manufacturer's instructions. Add meat and brown. Turn over and cook for recommended time.
(*U.S. Filet* – medium			2–3	
mignons) – well done			3	
Braising steak	16–17		10	Ideally cook on **Medium power**. If using **Full power**, leave to rest for 10 minutes halfway through the cooking time.
(*U.S. Chuck steak or blade beef*)				
Hamburgers 1 (100 g/4 oz)	—		2–3	Preheat the browning dish according to manufacturer's instructions. Add burgers and cook for recommended time, turning 100 g (4 oz) burgers over halfway through the cooking time and 225 g (8 oz) burgers over twice during the cooking time.
2 (100 g/4 oz)			3–4	
4 (100 g/4 oz)			5–6	
1 (225 g/8 oz)			2–3	
2 (225 g/8 oz)			6–7	
Lamb				
Leg – on bone	11–13		8–10	Choose a good quality joint. Roll into neat shape if off bone. Cover pointed end with foil to protect if on bone. Allow to stand for 25–30 minutes, wrapped in foil, before carving.
– off bone	12–13		9–10	
Breast	14–16		12	Roll and stuff if liked before cooking. Allow to stand for 30 minutes, in foil, before carving.
Crown roast	—		5	Cover tips of bone with foil during cooking.
Loin of lamb	11–13		8–10	Choose a good quality joint. Roll into neat shape if off bone. Cover pointed end with foil to protect if on bone. Allow to stand for 25–30 minutes, wrapped in foil, before carving.
Chops – loin or chump	2	—	6–7	Preheat the browning dish according to manufacturer's instructions. Add chops and cook for recommended time, turning over halfway through the cooking time.
	4	—	7–9	
Pork				
Leg	13–15		10	Choose a good quality joint. Cover pointed end with foil to protect from over-cooking. Score fat with a sharp knife and sprinkle liberally with salt to get a crisp crackling. Allow to stand for 20 minutes, wrapped in foil, before carving. Brown under a hot grill if liked.

64

Meat	Cooking time in minutes on Medium power per 450 g (1 lb)		Cooking time in minutes on Full power per 450 g (1 lb)	Guidelines
Boned loin (U.S. Boneless roast)		14–16	10–13	Roll into a neat shape before cooking. Allow to stand for 20 minutes, in foil, before carving.
Fillet (U.S. Pork tenderloin)		—	7	
Chops – loin or chump (U.S. Center cut pork chops)	2 3 4	14–18 19–24 26–32	—	Preheat the browning dish according to manufacturer's instructions. Add chops and cook for recommended time, turning over halfway through the cooking time.
Sausages (U.S. Pork sausage links)	2	— —	1½–2 3–3½	Prick thoroughly and arrange on a rack or plate. Cover with absorbent kitchen towel, turn halfway through cooking time.
Veal		11–12	8½–9	Secure into neat shape before cooking. Allow to stand 20 minutes, in foil, before carving.
Bacon, Ham or Gammon				
Joints (U.S. Roasts)		11–12	—	Secure into neat shape before cooking. Allow to stand 20 minutes, in foil, before carving.
Gammon steaks (each) (U.S. Bacon or ham steaks)			14	Cook in a browning dish if liked, observing preheating times, or cover with cling film. Turn over halfway through the cooking time.
Bacon – 4 slices 450 g (1 lb)		—	3½–4 12–14	Place on a plate or bacon rack and cover with absorbent kitchen towel. Turn rashers over halfway through the cooking time.
Offal (U.S. Variety meats)				
Liver		—	5–6	
Kidney		—	7–8	

Guide to defrosting poultry and game

Poultry and Game	Cooking time in minutes on Defrost power per 450 g (1 lb)	Preparation
Chicken (U.S. Chicken, Cornish hens and game hens)		
– whole	6	Shield the tips of the wings and legs with foil. Give the dish a quarter turn every 1½ minutes. Remove giblets at the end of the defrosting time.
– pieces	5	Place the meatiest part of the chicken piece to the outside of the dish. Turn over halfway through.
Duck	5–6	Shield the tips of the wings, tail and legs with foil. Give the dish a quarter turn every 1½ minutes. Remove giblets at the end of the defrosting time.
Grouse, Guinea fowl, Partridge, Pigeon, Pheasant, Quail, Poussin and Woodcock	5–6	Shield the tips of the wings and legs with foil. Turn over halfway through the defrosting time and give the dish a quarter turn every 1½ minutes.
Turkey	9–12	Shield the tips of wings and legs with foil. Turn over twice during defrosting time and give the dish a quarter turn every 6 minutes. Shield any warm spots with foil. Remove giblets at end of defrosting.

Note To defrost poultry and game on **Full power**, cook for 1 minute per 450 g (1 lb). Allow to stand for 10 minutes. Repeat until the poultry or game is thoroughly thawed.

Guide to roasting poultry and game

Poultry and Game	Cooking time in minutes on Full power per 450 g (1 lb)	Cooking time in minutes on Medium power per 450 g (1 lb)	Preparation
Chicken (U.S. Chicken, Cornish hens and game hens)			
– whole	6–7	8–10	Shield the tips of the wings and legs with foil. Place in a dish in a roaster bag with 3 tablespoons stock (U.S. ¼ cup bouillon). Give the dish a half turn halfway through the cooking time.
– pieces 1 2 3 4	2–4 4–6 5–7 6½–10		Place the meatiest part of the chicken piece to the outside of the dish. Cover with greaseproof paper. Give the dish a half turn halfway through the cooking time.
Duck – whole	6–8	10–11	Shield the tips of the wings, tail and legs with foil. Prick the skin thoroughly. Place in a dish in a roaster bag on a trivet or upturned saucer and turn over halfway through the cooking time.
Grouse, Guinea fowl, Partridge, Pheasant, Pigeon, Poussin, Quail and Woodcock	6–8	10–11	Shield the tips of the wings and legs with foil. Smear breast with a little butter. Place in a dish in a roaster bag. Turn the dish halfway through the cooking time.
Turkey	9–11	11–13	Shield the tips of the wings and legs with foil. Place in a dish in a roaster bag with 3 tablespoons stock (U.S. ¼ cup bouillon). Turn over at least once during the cooking time and give the dish a quarter turn every 15 minutes.

Lamb kebabs

(Illustrated on pages 62–63)

Power setting Full
Total cooking time 12–16 minutes

2 tablespoons (U.S. 3 tablespoons) oil
2 tablespoons (U.S. 3 tablespoons) red wine vinegar
$\frac{1}{2}$ teaspoon chopped fresh mixed herbs
$\frac{1}{4}$ teaspoon sugar
$\frac{1}{4}$ teaspoon dry mustard powder
1 clove garlic, crushed
salt and freshly ground black pepper
450 g/1 lb lean boneless lamb, cubed
4 lamb's kidneys, skinned, halved and cored
2 onions, peeled and thickly sliced
1 green pepper, seeds removed and sliced
4 tomatoes, halved
8 mushrooms, trimmed

Blend the oil with the wine vinegar, herbs, sugar, mustard, garlic and seasoning to taste. Place in a shallow dish, add the lamb and kidneys and leave to marinate for several hours.

Preheat a large browning dish or skillet for 5 minutes (or according to manufacturer's instructions). Place the drained lamb and kidneys on the dish, moving them around quickly on all sides to brown evenly.

Divide the lamb, kidney, onion, pepper, tomatoes and mushrooms evenly between four wooden skewers and brush with the marinade. Arrange in a large shallow dish and cook for 12–16 minutes. Baste the kebabs with any remaining marinade and give the dish a half turn halfway through the cooking time. Serve with boiled rice and salad.

Note: Metal skewers may be used in the microwave providing the food is packed tightly together so that the area of metal exposed is less than the area of food.
Serves 4

Redcurrant stuffed lamb

Power setting Full or Medium
Total cooking time about 40–50 or 52–65 minutes

1 (1.8–2.25 kg/4–5-lb) leg of lamb, boned
Stuffing
175 g/6 oz (U.S. 3 cups) fresh white breadcrumbs
4 tablespoons redcurrant preserve (U.S. $\frac{1}{3}$ cup redcurrant jelly)
2 tablespoons (U.S. 3 tablespoons) chopped parsley
grated rind of 1 lemon
25 g/1 oz (U.S. 2 tablespoons) butter, softened
2 small onions, peeled and finely chopped
100 g/4 oz (U.S. 1 cup) mushrooms, chopped
salt and freshly ground black pepper
1 egg, beaten

For the stuffing, mix the breadcrumbs with the redcurrant preserve, parsley, lemon rind, butter, onions, mushrooms and seasoning to taste. Bind together with the beaten egg. Spoon the stuffing firmly into the lamb and secure with string.

Weigh the stuffed lamb to calculate the precise cooking time. Place on a roasting rack or on an upturned saucer in a dish and cook on *Full Power* for 9–10 minutes per 450 g/1 lb or on *Medium Power* for 12–13 minutes per 450 g/1 lb. Wrap the lamb in foil and allow to stand for 30 minutes before carving to ensure any residual heat in the lamb is used.

Serve hot with vegetables in season or cold with salad, crusty bread and pickles. **Serves 6–8**

Lamb stuffed pancakes

Power setting Full
Total cooking time 9 minutes

450 g/1 lb minced lamb (U.S. 1 lb ground lamb)
grated rind of $\frac{1}{2}$ lemon
1 teaspoon dried thyme
1 (396-g/14 oz) can haricot beans, drained
1 clove garlic, crushed
salt and freshly ground black pepper
8 thin pancakes
150 ml/$\frac{1}{4}$ pint (U.S. $\frac{2}{3}$ cup) dry white wine
Garnish
tomato slices
parsley sprigs

Mix the lamb with the lemon rind, thyme, haricot beans, garlic and seasoning to taste. Cook for 3 minutes, stirring halfway through the cooking time.

Divide the mixture between the pancakes and roll up. Place side by side in a shallow dish. Pour over the wine and cover with cling film, snipping two holes in the top for the steam to escape. Cook for 3 minutes. Allow to stand for 3 minutes. Cook for a further 3 minutes.

Serve garnished with tomato slices and parsley sprigs. A tossed green salad makes a good accompaniment. **Serves 4**

Hunter's casserole

Power setting Full and Medium
Total cooking time 50 minutes

4 lamb shoulder chops
1 onion, peeled and sliced
1 green pepper, seeds removed and sliced
1 red pepper, seeds removed and chopped
2 tablespoons tomato purée (U.S. 3 tablespoons
tomato paste)
1 tablespoon brown sugar
$\frac{1}{2}$ teaspoon dry mustard powder
$\frac{1}{4}$ teaspoon salt
1 tablespoon horseradish sauce
2 tablespoons (U.S. 3 tablespoons) vinegar
600 ml/1 pint beef stock (U.S. $2\frac{1}{2}$ cups beef bouillon)

Place the lamb in a deep casserole with the onion, peppers, tomato purée, sugar, mustard, salt, horseradish sauce, vinegar and stock, mixing well. Cover and cook on *Full Power* for 10 minutes. Stir well to mix.

Cover and cook on *Medium Power* for 40 minutes, stirring halfway through the cooking time. Serve hot with boiled rice or pasta. **Serves 4**

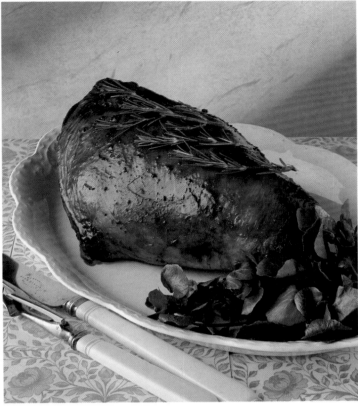

Curry and apple lamb

Power setting
Total cooking time 13–14 minutes

4 lamb leg steaks
Topping
25 g/1 oz (U.S. 2 tablespoons) butter
1 onion, peeled and finely chopped
1 large cooking apple, peeled, cored and chopped
1 teaspoon curry powder
2 teaspoons desiccated coconut (U.S. 2 teaspoons shredded coconut)
1 tablespoon chopped parsley
Garnish
halved tomatoes
watercress sprigs

Preheat a large browning dish or skillet for 5 minutes (or according to manufacturer's instructions). Add the steaks to the dish, moving them around quickly so that they brown evenly. Cook for 4 minutes. Turn the steaks over and cook for a further 4–5 minutes or until cooked. Cover with foil and leave to stand.

For the topping, place the butter in a bowl and cook for 1 minute to melt. Add the onion, apple and curry powder, cover and cook for 2 minutes. Add the coconut and parsley, and cook for a further 2 minutes.

Place the steaks on a heated serving plate. Top each steak with an equal quantity of the curry topping mixture. Serve garnished with halved tomatoes and watercress sprigs. **Serves 4**

Citrus leg of lamb

Power setting Full or Medium
Total cooking time 36–40 or 44–52 minutes

2 tablespoons (U.S. 3 tablespoons) soy sauce
1 tablespoon brown sugar
grated rind and juice of 1 lemon
salt and freshly ground black pepper
1 (1.8-kg/4-lb) leg of lamb
Garnish
rosemary sprigs
watercress sprigs

Mix the soy sauce, brown sugar, lemon rind and juice and seasoning to taste in a small bowl. Baste the lamb with a little of this marinade.

Place the lamb on a roasting rack or on an upturned saucer in a dish and cook on *Full Power* for 36–40 minutes or on *Medium Power* for 44–52 minutes. Baste three or four times and give the leg a half turn halfway through the cooking time.

Wrap the lamb in foil and allow to stand for 20 minutes before carving. Serve garnished with sprigs of rosemary and watercress. **Serves 6**

Super coconut lamb

Power setting Full
Total cooking time 13½–14½ minutes

4 lamb leg steaks
15 g/½ oz (U.S. 1 tablespoon) butter
100 g/4 oz (U.S. 1 cup) mushrooms, sliced
1 clove garlic, crushed
4 tomatoes, peeled and sliced
4 teaspoons desiccated coconut (U.S. 4 teaspoons shredded coconut)
mint sprigs to garnish

Preheat a large browning dish or skillet for 5 minutes (or according to the manufacturer's instructions). Add the steaks to the dish, moving them around quickly so that they brown evenly. Cook for 4 minutes. Turn the steaks over and cook for a further 4–5 minutes or until cooked. Cover with foil and leave to stand.

Place the butter in a bowl and cook for ½ minute to melt. Add the mushrooms and garlic, cover and cook for 2 minutes. Add the tomatoes and coconut, cover and cook for 3 minutes.

Place the steaks in a heated serving dish. Top with the tomato mixture. Brown further under a preheated hot grill if liked. Serve garnished with sprigs of mint. **Serves 4**

Variations
Super herby lamb Prepare and cook as above but use 4 teaspoons finely chopped fresh herbs instead of the desiccated coconut.
Super nutty lamb Prepare and cook as above but use 4 tablespoons (U.S ⅓ cup) coarsely chopped peanuts instead of the desiccated coconut.
Super cheesy lamb Prepare and cook as above but use 4 teaspoons grated Parmesan cheese instead of the desiccated coconut.
Super lemony lamb Prepare and cook as above but use the finely grated rind of ½ lemon instead of the desiccated coconut.
Super tomato and pepper coconut lamb Prepare as above but replace two of the tomatoes with 1 cored, seeded and sliced green pepper. Add the pepper with the tomatoes and coconut, cover and cook for 4–5 minutes.

Cheesy riblets of lamb with dates

Power setting Full and Medium
Total cooking time 18 minutes

225 g/8 oz (U.S. 1 cup) natural cottage cheese
2 tablespoons (U.S. 3 tablespoons) natural yogurt
1 teaspoon ground ginger
1 clove garlic, crushed (optional)
1 tablespoon ginger wine
salt and freshly ground black pepper
2 breasts of lamb
75 g/3 oz stoned dates (U.S. ½ cup pitted dates), coarsely chopped

Mix the cottage cheese with the yogurt, ginger, garlic if used, ginger wine and seasoning to taste. Chop the lamb breasts into riblets and place in a shallow dish with the cottage cheese mixture. Cover and leave to marinate for at least 2 hours.

Add the dates to the lamb mixture. Cook on *Full Power* for 4 minutes. Rearrange the lamb riblets and cook on *Medium Power* for 14 minutes until the ribs are cooked. Cover with foil and allow to stand for 10 minutes before serving. **Serves 4–6**

Apricot lamb

Power setting Full and Low
Total cooking time 1 hour–1 hour 10 minutes

1 (425-g/15-oz) can apricots, drained
350 g/12 oz (U.S. 1½ cups) pork sausagemeat
100 g/4 oz (U.S. 2 cups) fresh white breadcrumbs
salt and freshly ground black pepper
1 kg/2 lb boned shoulder of lamb
2 tablespoons (U.S. 3 tablespoons) oil
3 onions, peeled and sliced
4 stalks celery, chopped
600 ml/1 pint chicken stock (U.S. 2½ cups chicken
bouillon)
bouquet garni

Chop half of the apricots finely and mix with the sausagemeat, breadcrumbs and seasoning to taste. Place in the centre of the meat. Roll up and secure with string. Brush the meat with the oil.

Preheat a large browning dish or skillet for 5 minutes (or according to manufacturer's instructions). Place the lamb on the dish and roll around quickly to brown on all sides. Transfer to a shallow casserole.

Place the onions and celery around the meat and pour over the stock. Add the bouquet garni, cover and cook on *Full Power* for 20 minutes.

Add the remaining apricots, cover and cook on *Low Power* for 40–50 minutes until cooked and tender.

Remove and discard the bouquet garni. Cut the lamb into slices, garnish with parsley sprigs and serve with the cooked vegetables. Serve the flavoured stock as gravy separately. **Serves 4**

Variation
Peach and herby rice lamb Prepare and cook as above but use 65 g/2½ oz (U.S. ½ cup) cooked rice instead of the breadcrumbs. Use 350 g/12 oz (U.S. 1½ cups) herby sausagemeat instead of plain sausagemeat or add 2 teaspoons mixed dried herbs to the plain sausagemeat mixture, blending well. Substitute a drained 425-g/15-oz can peach slices for the canned apricots.

72

Marinated lamb hot pot

Power setting Full
Total cooking time 40 minutes

1 (1-kg/2-lb) loin of lamb, boned and rolled
150 ml/¼ pint (U.S. ⅔ cup) red wine
2 tablespoons (U.S. 3 tablespoons) oil
8 small onions, peeled
4 carrots, peeled and sliced
4 stalks celery, chopped
1 teaspoon dried oregano (optional)
salt and freshly ground black pepper
150 ml/¼ pint beef stock (U.S. ⅔ cup beef bouillon)
1 tablespoon flour
watercress sprigs to garnish

Marinate the lamb in the wine for at least 1 hour before cooking.

Remove the lamb from the wine and place with the oil in an oval, steep-sided glass dish. Cook for 7 minutes. Turn the meat over and cook for a further 5 minutes. Place the onions, carrots, celery, oregano and seasoning to taste around the lamb. Cover with cling film, snipping two holes in the top for the steam to escape. Cook for 25 minutes.

Remove the lamb and vegetables with a slotted spoon to a heated serving dish. Cover with foil.

Skim off any excess fat from the cooking juices. Dissolve the flour in a little of the wine then whisk into the cooking juices. Cook for 3 minutes, stirring every 1 minute to keep the sauce smooth.

Garnish the lamb with watercress sprigs and serve the sauce separately. **Serves 4–6**

Lamb with corn dumplings

Power setting Full and Medium
Total cooking time 1 hour–1 hour 5 minutes

450 g/1 lb lean boneless lamb, cut into bite-sized pieces
1 tablespoon flour
2 tablespoons (U.S. 3 tablespoons) oil
salt and freshly ground black pepper
450 g/1 lb (U.S. 3 cups) onions, peeled and sliced
1 teaspoon dried rosemary
450 ml/¾ pint beef stock (U.S. 2 cups beef bouillon)
100 g/4 oz (U.S. 1 cup) mushrooms, sliced
Corn dumplings
100 g/4 oz self-raising flour (U.S. 1 cup all-purpose flour sifted with 1 teaspoon baking powder)
50 g/2 oz (U.S. ⅓ cup) shredded beef suet
1 (198-g/7-oz) can sweetcorn kernels, drained
2 tablespoons (U.S. 3 tablespoons) chopped parsley

Place the meat in a casserole with the flour and toss to coat. Add the oil, seasoning to taste, onions, rosemary and beef stock. Mix well, cover and cook on *Full Power* for 10 minutes. Give the dish a half turn. Cook on *Medium Power* for 10 minutes. Give the dish a half turn, stir, re-cover and cook on *Medium Power* for a further 20 minutes.

Meanwhile for the dumplings, place the flour, suet, sweetcorn and parsley in a bowl. Season to taste and mix to a soft dough with water. Turn onto a floured surface and form into about 6 dumplings.

Stir the stew and add the mushrooms. Place the dumplings on top of stew and cook on *Medium Power* for 20–25 minutes. Allow to stand for 5 minutes before serving. **Serves 4**

Winter warming lamb

Power setting Full and Medium
Total cooking time 51 minutes

1 kg/2 lb middle neck of lamb (U.S. 2 lb lamb neck slices)
40 g/1½ oz (U.S. 6 tablespoons) flour
salt and freshly ground black pepper
2 tablespoons (U.S. 3 tablespoons) oil
2 onions, peeled and quartered
8 small carrots, peeled
2 stalks celery, sliced
450 ml/¾ pint beef stock (U.S. 2 cups beef bouillon)
½ head cauliflower, broken into florets
100 g/4 oz (U.S. ¾ cup) shelled peas

Toss the meat in the flour and seasoning to taste. Preheat a browning dish or skillet for 5 minutes (or according to manufacturer's instructions). Add the oil to the dish and cook on *Full Power* for 1 minute. Add the lamb, turning quickly on all sides to brown evenly. Cook on *Full Power* for 5 minutes.

Transfer to a large casserole and add the onions, carrots, celery, stock and seasoning to taste. Cover and cook on *Medium Power* for 35 minutes. Add the cauliflower and peas, cover and cook on *Medium Power* for a further 10 minutes. Allow to stand for 10 minutes before serving. **Serves 4–6**

Italian lamb casserole

Power setting Full and Medium
Total cooking time 47 minutes

675 g/1½ lb lean boneless lamb, cut into bite-sized pieces
40 g/1½ oz (U.S. 6 tablespoons) flour
2 teaspoons dried basil
salt and freshly ground black pepper
2 tablespoons (U.S. 3 tablespoons) oil
2 onions, peeled and chopped
1 (398-g/14-oz) can peeled tomatoes
250 ml/8 fl oz beef stock (U.S. 1 cup beef bouillon)
100 g/4 oz (U.S. 1 cup) cooked shell pasta
50 g/2 oz (U.S. ½ cup) cheese, grated

Toss the meat in the flour, basil and seasoning to taste. Preheat a browning dish or skillet for 5 minutes (or according to manufacturer's instructions). Add the oil to the dish and cook on *Full Power* for 1 minute. Add the lamb, turning quickly on all sides to brown evenly. Cook on *Full Power* for 5 minutes.

Transfer to a large casserole and add the onions, tomatoes with their juice, stock and seasoning to taste. Cover and cook on *Medium Power* for 35 minutes. Add the pasta, cover and cook on *Medium Power* for a further 3 minutes. Sprinkle with cheese and cook, uncovered, on *Medium Power* for a further 3 minutes or until the cheese melts. **Serves 4**

Lamb tandoori

Power setting Full
Total cooking time 7–9 minutes

4 lamb shoulder chops
Marinade
300 ml/½ pint (U.S. 1¼ cups) natural yogurt
½ teaspoon ground ginger
2 teaspoons paprika pepper
1 clove garlic, crushed
2 bay leaves
6 peppercorns
1 tablespoon tomato purée (U.S. 1 tablespoon tomato paste)
grated rind of 1 lemon
salt and freshly ground black pepper
Garnish
lemon slices
bay leaves

Mix together the yogurt, ginger, paprika, garlic, bay leaves, peppercorns, tomato purée, lemon rind and seasoning to taste. Pour over the chops in a shallow dish. Cover and leave to marinate for at least 2–3 hours. Remove the bay leaves and peppercorns and discard.

Preheat a large browning dish or skillet for 5 minutes (or according to manufacturer's instructions). Drain the lamb from the marinade and place on the dish. Cook for 4 minutes. Baste with the marinade, turn over and cook for a further 3–5 minutes. Baste with the marinade, twice during the last cooking period.

Serve the tandoori chops garnished with lemon slices and bay leaves. Boiled rice makes a good accompaniment. **Serves 4**

Peach and cider lamb special

**Power setting Full and Medium
Total cooking time 50 minutes**

2 tablespoons (U.S. 3 tablespoons) oil
25 g/1 oz plain flour (U.S. ¼ cup all-purpose flour)
1 shoulder lamb, boned and cubed
1 red pepper, seeds removed and chopped
1 green pepper, seeds removed and chopped
4 spring onions (U.S. 4 scallions), chopped
1 (425-g/15-oz) can peach slices in syrup
450 ml/¾ pint dry cider (U.S. 2 cups hard cider)
salt and freshly ground black pepper
100 g/4 oz (U.S. 2 cups) beansprouts

Mix the oil and flour together in a deep casserole. Cook on *Full Power* for 3 minutes until beige in colour. Add the lamb, stir and cook on *Full Power* for 5 minutes. Add the peppers, spring onions, peach slices and their syrup, cider and seasoning to taste. Cover and cook on *Medium Power* for 40 minutes.

Add the beansprouts, stir and cook on *Full Power* for 2 minutes. Serve with rice or pasta and a salad. **Serves 4**

Variations
Apricot and cider lamb special Prepare and cook as above but use 1 (425-g/15-oz) can apricot halves in syrup instead of the peach slices.
Peach and rabbit cider special Prepare and cook as above but use 675 g/1½ lb boneless rabbit cut into bite-sized pieces instead of the lamb.
Apple and lamb special Prepare and cook as above but use 450 ml/¾ pint (U.S. 2 cups) unsweetened apple juice instead of the cider and 4 peeled, cored and chopped cooking apples instead of the peaches. Add the chopped apple after cooking on *Medium Power* for 20 minutes.

Chinese style lamb

(Illustrated on pages 62–63)

Power setting Full
Total cooking time 22–24 minutes

1 (425-g/15-oz) can pineapple slices
1 onion, peeled and sliced
2 small carrots, peeled and sliced
100 g/4 oz (U.S. 1 cup) mushrooms, sliced
1 small green pepper, seeds removed and sliced
1 red pepper, seeds removed and sliced
1 tablespoon brown sugar
1 tablespoon soy sauce
2 tablespoons (U.S. 3 tablespoons) olive oil
3 tablespoons (U.S. $\frac{1}{4}$ cup) vinegar
1 tablespoon cornflour (U.S. 1 tablespoon cornstarch)
150 ml/$\frac{1}{4}$ pint chicken stock (U.S. $\frac{2}{3}$ cup chicken bouillon)
3 lamb double loin chops

Drain the pineapple, reserving the juice. Place the juice in a medium casserole with the onion, carrots, mushrooms and peppers. Cover and cook for 5 minutes.

Mix the brown sugar with the soy sauce, olive oil, vinegar and cornflour. Stir into the vegetables with the stock. Cover and cook for 8 minutes, stirring halfway through the cooking time. Set aside while you cook the meat.

Preheat a large browning dish or skillet for 5 minutes (or according to manufacturer's instructions). Place the chops on the dish and cook for 4 minutes. Turn over and cook for 3–5 minutes.

Place the chops in the sauce and cook for 2 minutes. Serve hot with the pineapple slices and boiled or stir-fried beansprouts. **Serves 3**

Navarin of lamb

Power setting Full and Low
Total cooking time 1 hour 19 minutes

1 kg/2 lb middle neck of lamb (U.S. 2 lb lamb neck slices)
2 tablespoons (U.S. 3 tablespoons) oil
1 onion, peeled and sliced
450 g/1 lb carrots, peeled and sliced
15 g/$\frac{1}{2}$ oz (U.S. 2 tablespoons) flour
450 ml/$\frac{3}{4}$ pint beef stock (U.S. 2 cups beef bouillon)
1 tablespoon tomato purée (U.S. 1 tablespoon tomato paste)
1 bouquet garni
8 new potatoes, peeled
salt and freshly ground black pepper
100 g/4 oz (U.S. $\frac{3}{4}$ cup) shelled peas

Preheat a large browning dish or skillet for 5 minutes (or according to manufacturer's instructions). Cut the lamb into single rib pieces. Place on the dish, moving them around quickly so that they brown evenly. Turn over and brown on the other sides. Set aside.

Place the oil in a deep casserole and cook on *Full Power* for 3 minutes. Add the sliced onion and carrots and cook on *Full Power* for 3 minutes. Remove with a slotted spoon. Add the flour and cook on *Full Power* for 3 minutes until beige in colour. Gradually add the stock, tomato purée, bouquet garni and lamb. Cover and cook on *Full Power* for 15 minutes. Add the cooked onion and carrots, new potatoes and seasoning to taste. Cover and cook on *Low Power* for 40 minutes. Add the peas and cook on *Low Power* for a further 15 minutes. Remove and discard the bouquet garni. Serve hot with crusty French bread. **Serves 4**

Baked meat loaf

Power setting Full
Total cooking time 13 minutes

1 tablespoon oil
1 onion, peeled and chopped
225 g/8 oz minced beef (U.S. ½ lb ground beef)
225 g/8 oz minced pork (U.S. ½ lb ground pork)
6 tablespoons (U.S. ½ cup) fresh brown breadcrumbs
1 clove garlic, crushed
1 tablespoon tomato purée (U.S. 1 tablespoon tomato paste)
salt and freshly ground black pepper
1 egg, beaten
Garnish
chopped parsley
watercress sprigs

Place the oil and onion in a bowl. Cover and cook for 3 minutes. Add the beef, pork, breadcrumbs, garlic, tomato purée and seasoning to taste. Bind together with the beaten egg. Pack into a greased 900-ml/2-pint (U.S 5-cup) loaf dish. Cook for 5 minutes. Cover with foil and leave to stand for 15 minutes.

Remove the foil and cook for a further 5 minutes. Cover with foil again and leave to stand for 5 minutes. Serve garnished with chopped parsley and watercress sprigs. Sliced tomatoes and new potatoes make good accompaniments. Alternatively, serve with a rich tomato sauce. **Serves 4**

Variations
Baked oatey meatloaf Prepare and cook as above but use 25 g/1 oz (U.S. ⅓ cup) rolled oats instead of half of the breadcrumbs.
Baked cheese and meat loaf Prepare and cook as above but place half of the meat mixture into the loaf dish. Top with 100 g/4 oz (U.S. 1 cup) grated cheese. Cover in turn with the remaining meat mixture, pressed down well. Cook as above but after removing the foil cook for a further 7 minutes. **Total cooking time 15 minutes**
Baked mushroom and meat loaf Prepare and cook as above but add 100 g/4 oz (U.S. 1 cup) cooked sliced mushrooms to the beef mixture.
Curried baked meatloaf Prepare and cook as above but add 1–2 teaspoons curry powder (to taste) to the beef mixture with 1 tablespoon raisins.

Summer beef steaks

Power setting Full
Total cooking time 20–27 minutes

6 rump steaks (U.S. 6 top round steaks)
150 ml/¼ pint (U.S. ⅔ cup) dry white wine
grated rind and juice of 1 lemon
2 tablespoons (U.S. 3 tablespoons) chopped fresh
mint, basil and parsley
freshly ground black pepper
1 tablespoon flour
2 teaspoons tarragon and thyme mustard
Garnish
fresh basil leaves
lemon rind

Place the steaks in a shallow dish with the wine, lemon rind and juice, herbs and pepper to taste. Leave to marinate for 2–3 hours.

Preheat a large browning dish or skillet for 5 minutes (or according to manufacturer's instructions). Place the drained steaks on the dish, cook for 18–24 minutes, according to taste, turning over halfway through the cooking time.

Pour the meat juices from the steaks into a jug. Mix with the flour and tarragon and thyme mustard. Gradually add the marinade. Cook for 2–3 minutes until thickened, stirring every 1 minute.

Garnish the steaks with the basil leaves and lemon rind and serve with the wine sauce. Boiled potatoes and mixed salad are excellent with this dish. **Serves 6**

Variation
Winter beef steaks Prepare and cook as above but use 150 ml/¼ pint (U.S. ⅔ cup) dry red wine instead of the white wine and 2 teaspoons dried mixed herbs instead of the fresh mint, basil and parsley. Garnish the steaks with parsley sprigs and lemon rind. Baked jacket potatoes and cooked tomatoes with vegetables in season make good accompaniments.

Chilli corn carne

(Illustrated on page 84)

**Power setting Full
Total cooking time 22 minutes**

2 tablespoons (U.S. 3 tablespoons) oil
1 large onion, peeled and chopped
2 cloves garlic, crushed
450 g/1 lb minced beef (U.S. 1 lb ground beef)
2 teaspoons chilli powder
¼ teaspoon dried oregano
1 teaspoon salt
4 tablespoons beef stock (U.S. ⅓ cup beef bouillon)
1 (398-g/14-oz) can peeled tomatoes
1 (340-g/12-oz) can sweetcorn kernels, drained
1 (432-g/15¼-oz) can red kidney beans, drained

Place the oil in a dish with the onion and garlic. Cover and cook for 2 minutes. Add the beef, cover and cook for 10 minutes, stirring halfway through the cooking time.

Stir in the chilli powder, oregano, salt, stock and tomatoes. Cover and cook for 5 minutes. Add the corn and kidney beans. Stir, cover and cook for 5 minutes.

Serve hot with crackers or boiled rice. **Serves 4**

Beef and bean hot pot

**Power setting Full and Low
Total cooking time 1 hour 8 minutes**

2 tablespoons (U.S. 3 tablespoons) oil
25 g/1 oz (U.S. ¼ cup) flour
2 teaspoons dry mustard powder
salt and freshly ground black pepper
450 g/1 lb braising steak (U.S. 1 lb chuck steak), cut into bite-sized pieces
1 small turnip, peeled and chopped
2 small swedes (U.S. 2 small rutabagas), peeled and quartered
225 g/8 oz (U.S. ½ lb) carrots, peeled and sliced
1 onion, peeled and sliced
300 ml/½ pint beef stock (U.S. 1¼ cups beef bouillon)
1 (220-g/7¾-oz) can baked beans
mint sprigs to garnish (optional)

Blend the oil, flour, mustard powder and seasoning to taste in a large deep dish. Cook on *Full Power* for 3 minutes. Add the steak, stir and cook on *Full Power* for 5 minutes. Add the turnip, swedes, carrots, onion and stock. Cover and cook on *Low Power* for 50 minutes, stirring occasionally. Add the beans, cover and cook on *Full Power* for 10 minutes.

Leave to stand, covered, for 15 minutes before serving. Garnish with a sprig of mint, if liked. **Serves 4**

Celebration turkey

(Illustrated on pages 62–63)

Power setting Full or Medium
Total cooking time about 1½ hours or 1 hour 50 minutes

1 (3.5-kg/8-lb) oven-ready turkey
25 g/1 oz (U.S. 2 tablespoons) butter
Stuffing
25 g/1 oz (U.S. ⅓ cup) rolled oats
50 g/2 oz (U.S. 1 cup) fresh brown breadcrumbs
1 small onion, peeled and grated
75 g/3 oz (U.S. ⅓ cup) cooked ham, finely chopped
2 stalks celery, finely chopped
1 tablespoon chopped parsley
½ teaspoon dried thyme
salt and freshly ground black pepper
1 egg, beaten
watercress sprigs to garnish

For the stuffing, mix the oats with the breadcrumbs, onion, ham, celery, parsley, thyme and seasoning to taste. Bind together with the beaten egg. Use to stuff the neck end of the turkey.

Weigh the turkey and calculate the cooking time at 12 minutes per 450 g/1 lb on *Medium Power* or 10 minutes per 450 g/1 lb on *Full Power*.

Rub the turkey skin with butter and protect the turkey wings with a little foil. Place on a roasting rack or upturned plate in a roasting bag, sealing the end with string or an elastic band. Cook for the calculated time, turning the dish three or four times during cooking.

Wrap the turkey in foil and leave to stand for 10–15 minutes before carving. Serve garnished with watercress sprigs. **Serves 8**

Mexican chicken

Power setting Full
Total cooking time 30½–34 minutes

4 chicken pieces
1 tablespoon oil
5 rashers streaky bacon (U.S. 5 bacon slices), rinds removed and chopped
1 onion, peeled and chopped
1 clove garlic, crushed
275 g/10 oz (U.S. 2 cups) tomatoes, peeled and chopped
1½ tablespoons (U.S. 2 tablespoons) chilli powder
½ teaspoon ground allspice
25 g/1 oz (U.S. 2 tablespoons) peanuts, coarsely chopped
40 g/1½ oz (U.S. ⅓ cup) almonds, coarsely chopped
2 tablespoons sesame seeds
300 ml/½ pint chicken stock (U.S. 1¼ cups chicken bouillon)
1 (340-g/12-oz) can sweetcorn kernels
25 g/1 oz plain chocolate (U.S. 1 tablespoon semi-sweet chocolate pieces)

Place the chicken in a dish with the meatiest parts to the outside of the dish. Cover with greaseproof paper and cook for 6½–10 minutes, giving the dish a half turn halfway through the cooking time. Set aside.

Place the oil in a casserole with the bacon, onion and garlic. Cover and cook for 7 minutes. Place in a blender with the tomatoes, chilli powder, allspice, peanuts, almonds, half the sesame seeds and a little of the stock. Purée until smooth.

Place this sauce in the casserole with the chicken, half of the corn and the chocolate. Cover and cook for 15 minutes, stirring halfway through the cooking time.

Place the remaining corn in a serving dish and cook for 2 minutes. Top with the Mexican chicken and sprinkle with the remaining sesame seeds.

Serve as part of a Mexican meal with Chilli corn carne and guacamole (made by blending 3 peeled, stoned and mashed avocados with 1 chopped green chilli, 1 tablespoon lemon juice, 25 g/1 oz (U.S. ½ cup) fresh white breadcrumbs, 1 tablespoon chopped onion, 1 (284-g/10-oz) can cream style corn, a dash of Tabasco sauce and seasoning to taste – illustrated opposite). **Serves 4**

Chicken and mushroom mould

Power setting Full
Total cooking time 7 minutes

225 g/8 oz (U.S. $\frac{1}{2}$ lb) large spinach leaves
25 g/1 oz (U.S. 2 tablespoons) butter
1 onion, peeled and finely chopped
100 g/4 oz (U.S. 1 cup) mushrooms, sliced
2 teaspoons dried oregano
salt and freshly ground black pepper
225 g/8 oz (U.S. 1 cup) cooked chicken, chopped
3 tomatoes, seeds removed and chopped
$\frac{1}{4}$ cucumber, finely chopped
175 g/6 oz (U.S. $1\frac{1}{2}$ cups) Edam cheese, finely grated
4 tablespoons (U.S. $\frac{1}{3}$ cup) mayonnaise

Wash the spinach leaves and without drying place in a polythene cookbag. Secure the end loosely with string or an elastic band. Cook for 3 minutes. Remove carefully and plunge into cold water to cool.

Line a 23-cm/9-inch sandwich tin with the spinach leaving enough hanging over the edges of the tin to cover the top of the filling.

Place the butter in a bowl with the onion, mushrooms, oregano and seasoning to taste. Cover and cook for 4 minutes. Allow to cool. When cold, mix with the chicken, tomatoes, cucumber, cheese and mayonnaise. Spoon into the spinach-lined tin. Cover with the overhanging spinach leaves and leave to set, about $1\frac{1}{2}$–2 hours.

To serve, unmould onto a serving plate and garnish with cucumber slices. Cut into wedges to serve.
Serves 6

Chicken drumstick and celery casserole

**Power setting Full
Total cooking time 22–24 minutes**

8 chicken drumsticks
1 tablespoon oil
4 stalks celery, sliced
1 (340-g/12-oz) can sweetcorn kernels with peppers
1 (295-g/10.4-oz) can condensed celery soup
120 ml/4 fl oz (u.s. ½ cup) water
Garnish
crushed potato crisps
chopped parsley

Place the chicken drumsticks in a dish with the meatiest parts to the outside of the dish. Brush each with a little of the oil. Cover and cook for 14 minutes. Give the dish a half turn halfway through the cooking time.

Place in a casserole with the celery, sweetcorn, soup and water. Cover and cook for 8–10 minutes until hot and bubbly. Serve the casserole garnished with crushed potato crisps and chopped parsley or parsley sprigs.
Serves 4–6

Variations
Chicken drumstick and mushroom casserole Prepare and cook as above but use 1 (295-g/10.4-oz) can condensed mushroom soup instead of celery soup.
Chicken drumstick and asparagus casserole Prepare and cook as above but use 1 (295-g/10.4-oz) can condensed asparagus soup instead of celery soup.
Chicken drumstick and tomato casserole Prepare and cook as above but use 1 (295-g/10.4-oz) can condensed cream of tomato soup instead of celery soup.

Chicken and cranberry vindaloo

Power setting Full
Total cooking time 22½–28 minutes

1 (1.5-kg/3-lb) chicken, cut into pieces
2 tablespoons (U.S. 3 tablespoons) oil
1 onion, peeled and chopped
1 packet Vindaloo curry mix
300 ml/½ pint (U.S. 1¼ cups) water
1 chicken stock cube (U.S. 1 chicken bouillon cube)
salt to taste
225 g/8 oz (U.S. ½ lb) cranberries

Place the chicken in a dish with the meatiest parts to the outside of the dish. Cover with greaseproof paper and cook for 6½–10 minutes, giving the dish a half turn halfway through the cooking time. Set aside.

Place the oil in a large casserole and add the onion. Cover and cook for 2 minutes. Add the curry mix. Cover and cook for 2 minutes. Gradually add the water, crumbled stock cube and salt to taste. Cover and cook for 4 minutes, stirring every 1 minute. Add the chicken pieces and cranberries. Cover and cook for 8–10 minutes.

Transfer to a heated serving dish on a bed of rice. Accompany with a cucumber raita salad and chapatis.
Serves 4

Bacon fricassée

Power setting Full
Total cooking time 11–12 minutes

50 g/2 oz (U.S. ¼ cup) butter
50 g/2 oz (U.S. ½ cup) flour
300 ml/½ pint (U.S. 1¼ cups) milk
150 ml/¼ pint (U.S. ⅔ cup) dry white wine
grated rind and juice of 1 orange
salt and freshly ground black pepper
450 g/1 lb cooked forehock bacon (U.S. 1 lb cooked smoked hock), cut into bite-sized pieces
2 rashers streaky bacon (U.S. 2 bacon slices), rinds removed
chopped parsley to garnish

Place the butter in a large jug and cook for 1 minute to melt. Add the flour and mix well. Gradually add the milk and wine, a little at a time. Cook for 4–4½ minutes, stirring every 1 minute until the sauce is smooth and thickened. Stir in the orange rind and juice and seasoning to taste. Mix with the bacon and place in a serving dish. Cook for 4 minutes until hot and bubbly.

Place the bacon rashers on a plate or roasting rack and cover with absorbent kitchen towel. Cook for 2–2½ minutes until crisp, turning the rashers over halfway through the cooking time. Chop coarsely and sprinkle over the top of the bacon fricassée. Serve garnished with chopped parsley. **Serves 6**

Summer pork casserole

Power setting Full
Total cooking time 23 minutes

450 g/1 lb potatoes, peeled and sliced
4 tablespoons (U.S. ⅓ cup) hot water
450 g/1 lb pork fillet (U.S. 1 lb pork tenderloin), cut
into bite-sized pieces
1 (396-g/14-oz) can peeled tomatoes
4–6 small leeks or 4 small courgettes (U.S. 4–6 small
leeks or 4 small zucchini), sliced
1 teaspoon finely chopped fresh basil
salt and freshly ground black pepper
100 g/4 oz (U.S. 1 cup) cheese, grated

Place the potatoes in a dish with the water. Cover and
cook for 6 minutes. Drain and remove the potatoes with
a slotted spoon.

Place the pork in a shallow serving dish. Cook for 5
minutes. Add the tomatoes, leeks or courgettes, basil
and seasoning to taste. Overlap the potatoes on top of
the meat mixture around the edge of the dish. Cook for
10 minutes or until the meat and potatoes are tender.

Cover the potatoes with the cheese. Cook for a
further 2 minutes. **Serves 4**

Cider apple chops

Power setting Medium and Full
Total cooking time 32–32½ minutes

salt and freshly ground black pepper
4 loin pork chops (U.S. 4 center cut pork chops)
25 g/1 oz (U.S. 2 tablespoons) butter
1 onion, peeled and chopped
1 cooking apple, peeled, cored and chopped
2 teaspoons lemon juice
1 tablespoon brown sugar
300 ml/½ pint (U.S. 1¼ cups) cider
1 tablespoon cornflour (U.S. 1 tablespoon cornstarch)
4 tablespoons double cream (U.S. ⅓ cup heavy cream)

Season the chops generously on both sides. Preheat a
large browning dish or skillet for 5 minutes (or
according to manufacturer's instructions) Add the
chops to the dish, moving them around quickly so that
they brown evenly. Cook for 13 minutes. Turn the
chops over, pointing the thin ends to the centre of the
dish. Cook for 7 minutes or until cooked. Cover with
foil and leave to stand.

Place the butter in a large bowl and cook for 1 minute
to melt. Add the onion and apple. Cover and cook for 4
minutes. Add the lemon juice, sugar and cider. Blend
the cornflour with a little water and stir into the sauce
mixture. Cook for 4–4½ minutes, stirring every 1
minute until the sauce is thickened. Blend in the cream.

Place the sauce in a shallow serving dish. Top with the
cooked chops and cook for 3 minutes. **Serves 4**

Caribbean pork curry

(Illustrated on pages 62–63)

Power setting Full
Total cooking time 46 minutes

1 tablespoon oil
1 large green pepper, seeds removed and finely sliced
1 large onion, peeled and sliced
1½ teaspoons turmeric
2 teaspoons salt
1 tablespoon curry powder (strength according to taste)
1 teaspoon ground cumin
1 teaspoon ground ginger
¾ teaspoon mild chilli powder
800 g/1¾ lb pork fillet (U.S. 1¾ lb pork tenderloin), cut into bite-sized pieces
25 g/1 oz (U.S. ¼ cup) flour
4 tomatoes, peeled and chopped
1 tablespoon tomato purée (U.S. 1 tablespoon tomato paste)
300 ml/½ pint chicken stock (U.S. 1¼ cups chicken bouillon)
1 (425-g/15-oz) can mango slices
100 g/4 oz (U.S. ¼ lb) fresh pineapple, chopped
50 g/2 oz (U.S. ⅓ cup) raisins
parsley sprigs to garnish

Place the oil, pepper, onion, turmeric, salt, curry powder, cumin, ginger and chilli powder in a large bowl. Cook, uncovered, for 7 minutes, stirring halfway through the cooking time.

Meanwhile, toss the pork in the flour until well coated. Add to the onion mixture, cover and cook for 24 minutes, stirring halfway through the cooking time.

Add the tomatoes, tomato purée and chicken stock, blending well. Cover and cook for 10 minutes. Add the mango slices with their juice, pineapple and raisins. Cover and cook for a further 5 minutes.

Serve the curry garnished with parsley sprigs. You can serve the curry with a selection of the following: cooked rice, poppadums, chapatis, mango chutney, cucumber raita salad and bhajis. **Serves 6**

Sweet and sour pork

Power setting Full
Total cooking time 10 minutes

4 tablespoons (U.S. ⅓ cup) oil
450 g/1 lb pork fillet (U.S. 1 lb pork tenderloin), cut into bite-sized pieces
5 tablespoons (U.S. 6 tablespoons) soy sauce
1 tablespoon cornflour (U.S. 1 tablespoon cornstarch)
2 tablespoons (U.S. 3 tablespoons) brown sugar
2 tablespoons (U.S. 3 tablespoons) white wine vinegar
2 tablespoons (U.S. 3 tablespoons) fresh orange juice
1½ tablespoons tomato purée (U.S. 2 tablespoons tomato paste)
1½ tablespoons (U.S. 2 tablespoons) dry sherry
100 g/4 oz (U.S. 1 cup) mushrooms, sliced
1 green pepper, seeds removed and sliced
1 (312-g/11-oz) can pineapple cubes, drained
Garnish
tomato roses
spring onion curls

Place the oil and pork into a large dish or casserole. Cover and cook for 4 minutes. Drain off any excess oil and add 3 tablespoons (U.S. 4 tablespoons) of the soy sauce. Cover and cook for 1 minute.

Blend the remaining soy sauce with the cornflour, sugar, vinegar, orange juice, tomato purée and sherry. Pour over the pork, add the mushrooms and stir to mix. Cook for 3 minutes, stirring halfway through the cooking time. Add the pepper and pineapple cubes. Cover and cook for a further 2 minutes. Allow to stand, covered, for 10 minutes.

Transfer the sweet and sour pork to a heated serving plate. Garnish with tomato roses and spring onion curls and serve with boiled rice. **Serves 6**

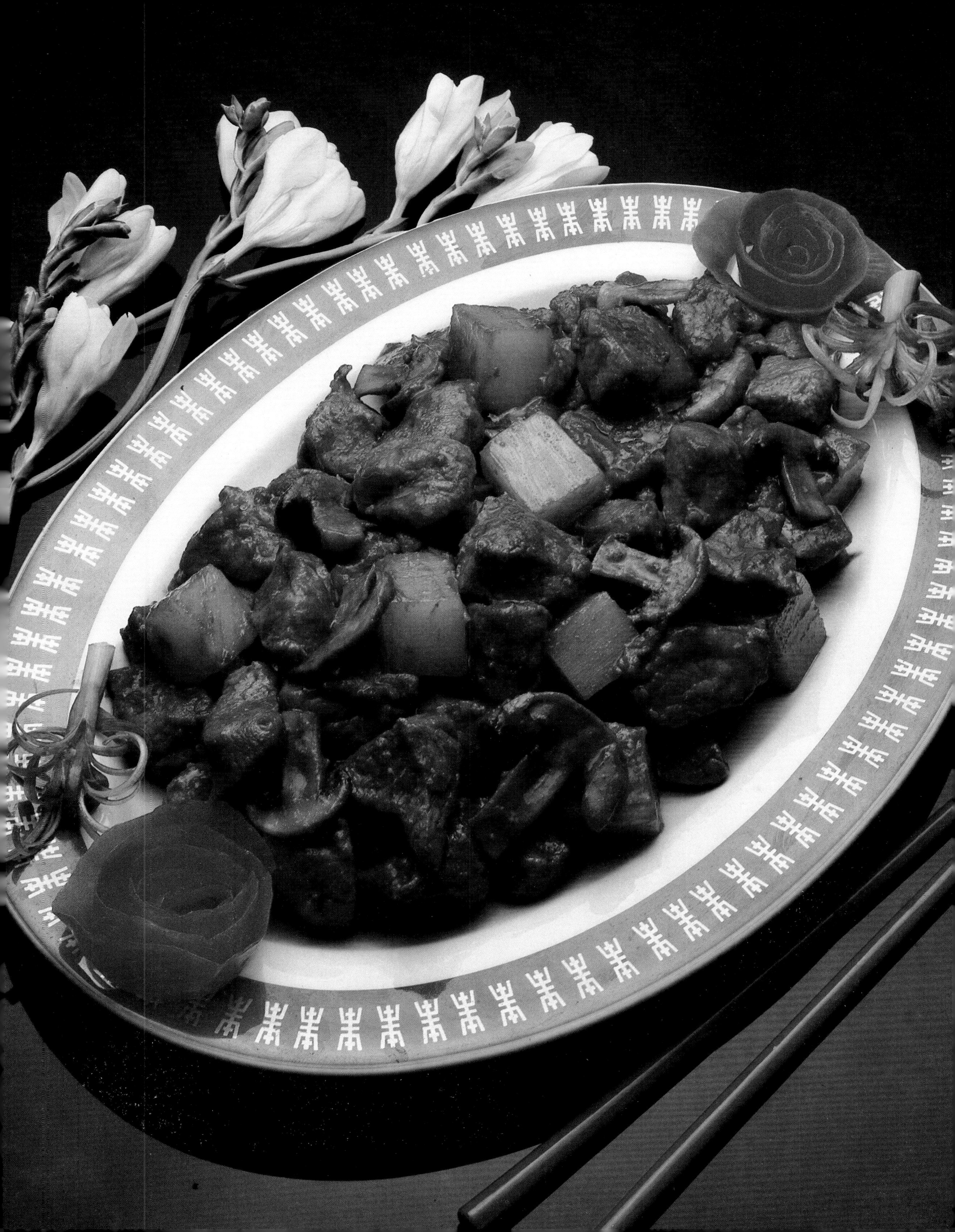

Liver and bacon crumble

Power setting Full
Total cooking time 25–27 minutes

3 tablespoons (U.S. ¼ cup) oil
450 g/1 lb lamb's liver, thinly sliced
6 rashers streaky bacon (U.S. 6 bacon slices), rinds
removed and chopped
2 leeks, thinly sliced
150 ml/¼ pint beef stock (U.S. ⅔ cup beef bouillon)
Crumble topping
75 g/3 oz plain flour (U.S. ¾ cup all-purpose flour)
1 teaspoon dry mustard powder
salt and freshly ground black pepper
50 g/2 oz (U.S. ¼ cup) butter
25 g/1 oz (U.S. ¼ cup) Cheddar cheese, grated
25 g/1 oz (U.S. ¼ cup) rolled oats
sliced tomatoes to garnish

Place the oil in a dish and cook for 1 minute. Add the liver and cook for 5 minutes, turning over halfway through the cooking time. Remove with a slotted spoon and set aside. Add the bacon and cook for 5 minutes. Remove with a slotted spoon and set aside. Add the leeks to the juices, cover and cook for 3 minutes. Layer the liver, bacon and leeks in a pie dish and pour over the stock.

For the crumble topping, sift the flour with the mustard powder and seasoning to taste. Rub in the butter until the mixture resembles fine breadcrumbs. Stir in the cheese and oats, blending well.

Spoon the crumble topping carefully on top of the liver mixture. Cook for 11–13 minutes, giving the dish a quarter turn every 3 minutes. Place under a preheated hot grill to brown further if liked. Serve garnished with sliced tomatoes. **Serves 4**

Liver provençal

Power setting Full
Total cooking time 13 minutes

25 g/1 oz (U.S. 2 tablespoons) butter
1 tablespoon oil
1 clove garlic, crushed
1 green pepper, seeds removed and sliced
100 g/4 oz (U.S. 1 cup) mushrooms, sliced
450 g/1 lb lamb's liver, finely sliced
4 large tomatoes, peeled and chopped
2 teaspoons brown sugar
2 teaspoons lemon juice or vinegar
1 teaspoon dried oregano
dash of Tabasco sauce
2 teaspoons cornflour (U.S. 2 teaspoons cornstarch)
parsley sprigs to garnish

Place the butter and oil in a casserole and cook for 1 minute to melt. Add the garlic, pepper and mushrooms and cook for 3 minutes. Add the liver, tomatoes, sugar, lemon juice or vinegar, oregano and Tabasco sauce, mixing well. Cover and cook for 5 minutes, stirring halfway through the cooking time.

Mix the cornflour with a little water and stir into liver mixture. Cover and cook for a further 4 minutes, stirring every 1 minute. Allow to stand for 10 minutes. Garnish with parsley sprigs and serve with herbed pasta.
Serves 4

Frankfurter cassoulet

Power setting Full and Low
Total cooking time 50 minutes

450 g/1 lb frankfurters, cut into bite-sized pieces
450 g/1 lb belly of pork (U.S. 1 lb fresh pork sides),
cut into bite-sized pieces
1 (425-g/15-oz) can peeled tomatoes
1 (425-g/15-oz) can cannellini beans, drained
1 (425-g/15-oz) can red kidney beans, drained
1 clove garlic, crushed
2 onions, peeled and sliced
4 stalks celery, sliced
1 tablespoon Worcestershire sauce
1½ tablespoons (U.S. 2 tablespoons) brown sugar
2 tablespoons (U.S. 3 tablespoons) flour
600 ml/1 pint chicken stock (U.S. 2½ cups chicken
bouillon)

Place the frankfurters, pork, tomatoes, cannellini beans, kidney beans, garlic, onions, celery, Worcestershire sauce and brown sugar in a large casserole. Mix the flour with a little of the stock and stir into the casserole ingredients. Add the remaining stock, mixing well to blend. Cover and cook on *Full Power* for 10 minutes. Stir well, cover and cook on *Low Power* for a further 40 minutes, stirring occasionally.

Leave the dish to stand, covered, for 10 minutes. Serve with crusty bread and/or vegetables in season. **Serves 6**

Variation
Crusty frankfurter cassoulet Prepare and cook as above and leave to stand, covered for 10 minutes. Remove the cover and sprinkle with a mixture of 2 tablespoons (U.S. 3 tablespoons) grated cheese and 4 tablespoons (U.S. ⅓ cup) fresh white breadcrumbs. Brown under a preheated hot grill until golden, bubbly and crisp.

Barbecue beans and bangers

Power setting Full
Total cooking time 14½–15 minutes

450 g/1 lb sausages (U.S. 1 lb sausage links)
knob of butter
2 (425-g/15-oz) cans baked beans
1½ tablespoons (U.S. 2 tablespoons)
Worcestershire sauce
2 tablespoons (U.S. 3 tablespoons) brown sauce
2 tablespoons (U.S. 3 tablespoons) brown sugar
1 small onion, peeled and chopped

Prick the sausages thoroughly with the prongs of a fork. Preheat a large browning dish or skillet for 5 minutes (or according to manufacturer's instructions). Quickly add the butter to the dish and swirl to coat. Add the sausages and turn over to brown on both sides. Cook for 6½–7 minutes, turning and rearranging halfway through the cooking time.

Meanwhile, mix the baked beans with the Worcestershire sauce, brown sauce, sugar and onion. Place in a large casserole dish with the cooked sausages. Cover and cook for 8 minutes until hot and bubbly. **Serves 4**

Variations
Curried beans and bangers Prepare and cook as above but use 2–3 teaspoons curry powder, strength according to taste, instead of the Worcestershire sauce and 1 tablespoon mango chutney instead of the brown sauce.
Barbecue beans and bangers with herby cobbler topping Prepare and cook the barbecue beans and bangers as above. Meanwhile, sift 225 g/8 oz self-raising flour (U.S. 2 cups all-purpose flour sifted with 2 teaspoons baking powder) into a bowl. Rub in 50 g/2 oz (U.S. ¼ cup) butter until the mixture resembles fine breadcrumbs. Add 1 beaten egg and 5 tablespoons (U.S. 6 tablespoons) milk and 2 teaspoons mixed dried herbs and mix to form a fairly soft dough. Roll out on a lightly floured surface to about 2 cm (¾ inch) thick. Cut out about 16 (5-cm/2-inch) rounds with a scone or biscuit cutter. Place on a large greased plate or microwave tray and cook, uncovered, on *Full Power* for 6–8 minutes until cooked. Place on top of the barbecue beans and bangers to serve.

Eggs and Cheese

Eggs and cheese must be the two most versatile foods for preparing quick snacks, delicious main meals and tasty supper dishes. The microwave will make them seem more so – imagine creamy scrambled eggs in literally seconds and bubbly savoury rarebits in minutes – the speed is hard to beat.

When cooking eggs in the microwave it is important to remember that the yolks cook faster than the whites. For this reason it is recommended that the yolks of whole eggs should be pricked lightly with a cocktail stick prior to cooking. This provides an outlet for the pressure that builds up during cooking and will not affect the end result or appearance of the egg after cooking.

Cheese also attracts microwave energy readily so take care not to overcook or it will become hard and stringy. And only add grated cheese toppings to main dishes during the last few minutes of the cooking time for perfect just-melted results.

If you enjoy cheese dishes with a golden-brown crust then quickly flash under a pre-heated hot grill before serving.

Scrambled eggs

Power setting Full
Total cooking time $4\frac{3}{4}$–5 minutes

25 g/1 oz (U.S. 2 tablespoons) butter
4 eggs, beaten
4 tablespoons (U.S. $\frac{1}{3}$ cup) milk
salt and freshly ground black pepper

Place the butter in a dish and cook for 1 minute to melt. Mix the eggs with the milk and seasoning to taste. Add to the butter and cook for 2 minutes. Stir well and cook for a further $1\frac{3}{4}$–2 minutes, stirring halfway through the cooking time. Allow to stand for 1–2 minutes to cook with the residual heat before serving. **Serves 4**

To cook less or more than four scrambled eggs, follow the chart below:

Eggs	Butter	Milk	Cooking Time
1	1 teaspoon	1 tablespoon	$\frac{3}{4}$–1 minute
2	2 teaspoons	2 tablespoons (U.S. 3 tablespoons)	$1\frac{3}{4}$–2 minutes
3	1 tablespoon	3 tablespoons (U.S. $\frac{1}{4}$ cup)	$2\frac{1}{2}$–$2\frac{3}{4}$ minutes
6	2 tablespoons (U.S. 3 tablespoons)	6 tablespoons (U.S. $\frac{1}{2}$ cup)	$5\frac{1}{2}$–6 minutes

Baked eggs

Power setting Medium
Total cooking time $3\frac{1}{2}$–4 minutes

butter to grease
4 eggs

Well butter four small glass cups or four cups in a microwave bun tray or muffin pan. Crack the eggs into the prepared dishes and carefully puncture each yolk with the tip of a sharp knife to prevent bursting during cooking. Cover with cling film, snipping two holes in the top for the steam to escape. Cook for $3\frac{1}{2}$–4 minutes, giving the dish a half turn after 2 minutes. **Serves 4**

To cook less or more than four eggs, follow the chart below:

Eggs	Cooking Time
1	1–$1\frac{1}{4}$ minutes
2	2–$2\frac{1}{4}$ minutes
3	3–$3\frac{1}{4}$ minutes
6	$5\frac{1}{2}$–6 minutes

Poached eggs

Power setting Full
Total cooking time $6\frac{1}{2}$–8 minutes

475 ml/16 fl oz (U.S. 2 cups) hot water
2 teaspoons vinegar
4 eggs

Place 120 ml/4 fl oz (U.S. $\frac{1}{2}$ cup) water in each of four small cocottes or dishes. Add a little of the vinegar. Cook for 4–5 minutes until the water and vinegar mixture boils. Carefully break an egg into each dish and puncture the yolk quickly with the tip of a sharp knife. Cook for $2\frac{1}{2}$–3 minutes, giving the dishes a half turn after $1\frac{1}{2}$ minutes. **Serves 4**

To cook less or more than four poached eggs. Place 120 ml/4 fl oz (U.S. $\frac{1}{2}$ cup) water in each container. Bring to the boil by cooking for $1\frac{1}{2}$ minutes each. Add the eggs as before and cook for the following times:

Eggs	Cooking Time
1	$\frac{3}{4}$–1 minute
2	1–$1\frac{1}{2}$ minutes
3	$1\frac{1}{2}$–$2\frac{1}{2}$ minutes
6	$4\frac{1}{2}$–5 minutes

Fried eggs

Power setting Full
Total cooking time 2–$2\frac{1}{4}$ minutes

25 g/1 oz (U.S. 2 tablespoons) butter
4 eggs

Preheat a flat-based browning dish or skillet for 4 minutes (or according to the manufacturer's instructions). Add the butter and swirl to coat the base. Crack the eggs onto the dish. Cover and cook for 2–$2\frac{1}{4}$ minutes. **Serves 4**

To cook less or more than four eggs, preheat the browning dish as above, then follow the chart below:

Eggs	Cooking Time
1	40–50 seconds
2	$1\frac{1}{2}$–$1\frac{3}{4}$ minutes
3	$1\frac{3}{4}$–2 minutes
6	$3\frac{3}{4}$–$3\frac{1}{2}$ minutes

Piperade

Power setting Full
Total cooking time 16–16½ minutes

1 tablespoon oil
1 large onion, peeled and sliced
4 green peppers, seeds removed and sliced
675 g/1½ lb tomatoes, peeled, seeds removed and
chopped
1 clove garlic, crushed
1 tablespoon chopped fresh basil
salt and freshly ground black pepper
4 eggs, beaten
parsley sprigs to garnish

Place the oil in a dish with the onion and peppers. Cover and cook for 6 minutes. Add the tomatoes, garlic, basil and seasoning to taste. Cook for 6 minutes until pulpy, stirring halfway through the cooking time.

Add the beaten eggs and cook for a further 4–4½ minutes or until the eggs are just lightly scrambled. Garnish with parsley sprigs and serve at once. **Serves 4**

Speedy Spanish omelette

Power setting Full
Total cooking time 7¾–8¼ minutes

1 onion, peeled and chopped
40 g/1½ oz (U.S. 3 tablespoons) butter
1 small red pepper, seeds removed and chopped
1 large cooked potato, chopped
1 tomato, peeled and chopped
½ teaspoon dried thyme
salt and freshly ground black pepper
4 eggs, beaten
3 tablespoons (U.S. ¼ cup) milk

Place the onion and 25 g/1 oz (U.S. 2 tablespoons) of the butter in a bowl and cook for 2 minutes. Add the red pepper and cook for a further 2 minutes. Add the potato, tomato, thyme and seasoning to taste.

Beat the eggs with the milk and add the vegetable mixture. Place the remaining butter in a 25-cm/10-inch pie plate and cook for ½ minute to melt. Swirl over the base to completely coat. Pour in the egg and vegetable mixture. Cover with cling film, snipping two holes in the top for the steam to escape. Cook for 1½ minutes then, using a spatula, move the cooked egg from the edge of the dish to the centre. Re-cover and cook for a further 1¾–2¼ minutes. Allow to stand for about 2 minutes before serving garnished with parsley sprigs and cut into wedges. **Serves 2**

Bacon and egg snack

Power setting Full
Total cooking time $5\frac{1}{2}$–$6\frac{1}{4}$ minutes

4 rashers back bacon (U.S. 4 slices Canadian bacon),
rinds removed and chopped
2 eggs, beaten
salt and freshly ground black pepper
$\frac{1}{2}$ teaspoon Worcestershire sauce
1 slice toast
Garnish
tomato slices
mustard and cress

Place the chopped bacon in a bowl and cook for $3\frac{1}{2}$–4 minutes until crisp.

Beat the eggs with seasoning to taste and the Worcestershire sauce. Pour into the bacon, mixing well. Cover and cook for 2–$2\frac{1}{4}$ minutes, stirring halfway through the cooking time. Pile onto the toast. Garnish with tomato slices and mustard and cress. **Serves 1**

Hungry eggs

Power setting Full and Medium
Total cooking time $8\frac{1}{2}$–10 minutes

1 (213-g/$7\frac{1}{2}$-oz) can butter beans, drained
2 tomatoes, peeled and chopped
salt and freshly ground black pepper
25 g/1 oz (U.S. 2 tablespoons) butter
4 eggs
4 thick slices buttered toast
paprika pepper
parsley sprigs to garnish

Place the beans in a bowl with the tomatoes, seasoning to taste and butter. Cook on *Full Power* for 5–6 minutes, stirring halfway through the cooking time.

Crack the eggs into a buttered microwave bun tray or 4 buttered small glass cups. Puncture the yolks carefully with the tip of a sharp knife to prevent bursting during cooking. Cover with cling film, snipping two holes in the top for the steam to escape. Cook on *Medium Power* for 2 minutes. Give the dish a half turn and cook for a further $1\frac{1}{2}$–2 minutes.

Spoon the beans over the toast and top with the baked eggs. Sprinkle with paprika and garnish with parsley sprigs. **Serves 4**

Egg and chicken pie

Power setting Full
Total cooking time 16½–18 minutes

50 g/2 oz (u.s. ¼ cup) butter
1 onion, peeled and chopped
100 g/4 oz (u.s. 1 cup) mushrooms, sliced
225 g/8 oz (u.s. ½ lb) cooked chicken, cut into
bite-sized pieces
4 tomatoes, peeled and chopped
4 hard-boiled eggs (u.s. 4 hard-cooked eggs), shelled
and sliced
25 g/1 oz (u.s. ¼ cup) flour
300 ml/½ pint hot chicken stock (u.s. 1¼ cups hot
chicken bouillon)
1 egg yolk
1 tablespoon chopped parsley
1 teaspoon dried tarragon
salt and freshly ground black pepper
1 (370-g/13-oz) packet frozen puff pastry, thawed
beaten egg to glaze

Place half the butter in a bowl with the onion. Cover
and cook for 2 minutes. Add the mushrooms, cover and
cook for a further 2 minutes. Add the chicken, tomatoes
and eggs and place in a large pie dish.

Place the remaining butter in a jug and cook for 1
minute to melt. Add the flour, blending well. Gradually
add the hot stock. Cook for 3½–4 minutes, stirring every
1 minute until the sauce is smooth and thickened. Allow
to cool slightly then add the egg yolk, parsley, tarragon
and seasoning to taste. Pour the sauce over the chicken
and egg mixture.

Roll out the pastry on a lightly floured surface and
use to make a pie lid about 2.5 cm/1 inch larger than the
pie dish. Brush the edges of the pie dish with beaten egg.
Place the pastry over the dish, folding the edges under to
form a double thickness. Knock up and flute the edges
decoratively. Make several cuts in the pie crust for the
steam to escape. Decorate with any pastry trimmings as
liked. Glaze with beaten egg and cook for 8–9 minutes
until the pastry is well risen and holding its shape. Place
under a preheated hot grill until golden. **Serves 4**

Cheesy stuffed pears

Power setting Full
Total cooking time 7–8 minutes

3 ripe dessert pears, peeled, cored and halved
4 tablespoons (u.s. ⅓ cup) water
2 teaspoons lemon juice
175 g/6 oz (u.s. ¾ cup) herb and garlic cream cheese
6 tablespoons (u.s. ½ cup) natural yogurt
salt and freshly ground black pepper
100 g/4 oz (u.s. ¼ lb) Stilton cheese
50 g/2 oz (u.s. ¼ cup) butter
watercress sprigs to serve

Place the pears in a shallow dish in one layer with the
water and lemon juice. Cover and cook for 7–8 minutes
until tender. Allow to cool completely then drain.

Mix the cream cheese with the yogurt and seasoning
to taste to produce a smooth thick sauce. Mash the
Stilton with the butter until well blended. Fill the pear
cavities with the Stilton mixture and place on a bed of
watercress. Pour over the cream cheese dressing and
serve chilled. **Serves 6**

Speedy cheese and tuna pizza

Power setting Full
Total cooking time 18–22 minutes

Bases
350 g/12 oz self-raising flour (U.S. 3 cups all-purpose
flour sifted with 2 teaspoons baking powder)
½ teaspoon salt
1 teaspoon baking powder
75 g/3 oz (U.S. 6 tablespoons) butter
75 g/3 oz (U.S. ¾ cup) cheese, grated
150 ml/¼ pint (U.S. ⅔ cup) milk
Topping
1 recipe Quick tomato sauce – chunky (see page 125)
1 (198-g/7-oz) can tuna fish, drained
2 teaspoons dried oregano
100 g/4 oz (U.S. 1 cup) cheese, grated
2 (56-g/2-oz) cans anchovy fillets, drained
black olives (U.S. ripe olives) to garnish (optional)

Sift the flour with the salt and baking powder into a
bowl. Rub in the butter until the mixture resembles fine
breadcrumbs. Stir in the cheese and milk and bind to a
soft scone dough. Divide into four portions and roll out
each to a 20-cm/8-inch round. Place on individual
greased plates.

Top each pizza with an equal quantity of the chunky
tomato sauce, flaked tuna, sprinkling of oregano, cheese
and a lattice of anchovy fillets. Garnish with black olives
if liked. Cook each pizza separately for 4½–5½ minutes,
giving the dish a quarter turn every 1 minute. **Serves 4**

Variations
Mushroom pizzas Prepare and cook as above but
sprinkle each pizza with 50 g/2 oz (U.S. ½ cup) sliced
mushrooms instead of the tuna.
Ham pizzas Prepare and cook as above but top each
pizza with 50 g/2 oz (U.S. ¼ cup) chopped cooked ham
instead of the tuna.
Salami pizzas Prepare and cook as above but top each
pizza with 6–8 slices salami instead of the tuna.

Quiche Lorraine

Power setting Full and Defrost
Total cooking time 20½–24 minutes

Pastry
175 g/6 oz plain flour (U.S. 1½ cups all-purpose flour)
pinch of salt
75 g/3 oz (U.S. 6 tablespoons) butter
3 tablespoons (U.S. ¼ cup) water
Filling
4 rashers back bacon (U.S. 4 slices Canadian bacon),
rinds removed and chopped
50 g/2 oz (U.S. ½ cup) cheese, grated
2 eggs, beaten
1 egg yolk
salt and freshly ground black pepper
150 ml/¼ pint single cream (U.S. ⅔ cup light cream)
2 teaspoons chopped parsley
Garnish
tomato slices
parsley sprigs

Sift the flour with the salt into a bowl. Rub in the butter
until the mixture resembles fine breadcrumbs. Stir in
the water and mix well to bind. Roll out the pastry on a
lightly floured surface to a round large enough to line a
20-cm/8-inch flan dish. Press in firmly taking care not
to stretch the pastry. Cut the pastry away leaving a
5 mm/¼ inch 'collar' above the dish (this allows for any
shrinkage that may occur). Prick the base well with a
fork. Line the inside, upright edge of the pastry case
with a long strip of foil, about 4 cm/1½ inches wide.
(This prevents the outer edges from overcooking.) Place
a double thickness layer of absorbent kitchen towel over
the base, easing into position around the edges to keep
the foil in place. Cook on *Full Power* for 4–4½ minutes,
giving the dish a quarter turn every 1 minute. Remove
the paper and foil and cook on *Full Power* for a further
1–2 minutes. Allow to cool.

Meanwhile, for the filling, place the bacon in a bowl
and cook on *Full Power* for 1½ minutes. Drain and place
in the base of the flan case. Top with the cheese. Beat the
eggs with the egg yolk, seasoning to taste and the cream.
Pour into the flan case and sprinkle with the parsley.

Cook on *Defrost Power* for 14–16 minutes, giving the
dish a quarter turn every 3 minutes. Allow to stand for
15–20 minutes. The flan should set completely during
this time. If not quite set then cook for an extra ½–1
minute. Garnish with tomato slices and parsley sprigs.
Serves 4–6

Leicestershire rarebit crumpets

Power setting Full and Medium
Total cooking time 7–10 minutes

225 g/8 oz (U.S. 2 cups) Leicestershire cheese, grated
15 g/½ oz (U.S. 1 tablespoon) butter
2 teaspoons made mustard
3 tablespoons double cream (U.S. ¼ cup heavy cream)
1 egg yolk
salt and freshly ground black pepper
4 toasted and buttered crumpets or bread rolls
Garnish
watercress sprigs (optional)
tomato slices (optional)

Place the cheese and butter in a bowl and cook on *Full Power* for 2–3 minutes, stirring every 1 minute until the cheese has melted to a smooth sauce.

Add the mustard, cream, egg yolk and seasoning to taste. Cook on *Medium Power* for 5–7 minutes until hot and very smooth. Pour over the toasted crumpets or rolls and serve. Garnish with watercress sprigs and tomato slices if liked. **Serves 4**

Cheese and potato bake

Power setting Full
Total cooking time 17 minutes

25 g/1 oz (U.S. 2 tablespoons) butter
1 large onion, peeled and chopped
675 g/1½ lb potatoes, peeled and thinly sliced
75 g/3 oz (U.S. ¾ cup) cheese, grated
salt and freshly ground black pepper
150 ml/¼ pint (U.S. ⅔ cup) milk
parsley sprigs to garnish

Place the butter in a bowl with the onion. Cook for 3 minutes, stirring halfway through the cooking time.

Place a layer of potatoes in the base of a shallow dish. Top with a little cheese, a little onion and seasoning. Continue to layer the potatoes, cheese and onion, seasoning generously between each, finishing with a layer of potato and cheese. Pour over the milk, cover with cling film, snipping two holes in the top for the steam to escape. Cook for 7 minutes.

Remove the cling film, give the dish a half turn and cook for a further 7 minutes. Allow to stand for 5 minutes before serving. Brown under a preheated hot grill if liked. Garnish with parsley sprigs. **Serves 4**

Belgian chicory, ham and cheese roulades

Power setting Full
Total cooking time 15–17½ minutes

8 heads of chicory (8 heads of Belgian endive), trimmed
2 tablespoons (U.S. 3 tablespoons) lemon juice
150 ml/¼ pint (U.S. ⅔ cup) water
8 slices cooked ham
25 g/1 oz (U.S. 2 tablespoons) butter
40 g/1½ oz plain flour (U.S. 6 tablespoons all–purpose flour)
300 ml/½ pint (U.S. 1¼ cups) milk
50 g/2 oz (U.S. ½ cup) Gruyère cheese, grated
25 g/1 oz (U.S. ¼ cup) Parmesan cheese, grated

Place the chicory in a dish with the lemon juice and water. Cover and cook for 7–8 minutes, re-arranging halfway through the cooking time. Drain and wrap each head of chicory in the ham. Place side by side in a serving dish.

Place the butter in a large jug and cook for 1 minute to melt. Add the flour and mix well. Gradually add the milk, a little at a time. Cook for 4–4½ minutes, stirring every 1 minute until the sauce is smooth and thickened. Stir in the cheeses and allow to melt. Pour over the ham roulades. Cook for 3–4 minutes until hot and bubbly. Brown under a preheated hot grill if liked. **Serves 4**

Gouda cheese fondue

Power setting Full and Medium
Total cooking time 6–7½ minutes

½ clove garlic, crushed
150 ml/¼ pint (U.S. ⅔ cup) medium dry cider, lager or dry white wine
1 teaspoon lemon juice
1½ tablespoons (U.S. 2 tablespoons) gin or Kirsch
400 g/14 oz (U.S. 3½ cups) Gouda cheese, grated
1 tablespoon cornflour (U.S. 1 tablespoon cornstarch)
pinch of ground nutmeg
freshly ground black pepper
cubes of French bread to serve

Place the garlic, cider, lager or wine, lemon juice and gin or Kirsch in a fondue dish or casserole. Cook on *Full Power* for 3½–4 minutes until very hot.

Toss the cheese with the cornflour, nutmeg and pepper to taste until well blended. Quickly stir or whisk the cheese into the hot liquid and cover. Cook on *Medium Power* for 2½–3½ minutes, stirring every 1 minute until the cheese is just melted.

Serve at once with cubes of crusty French bread for dipping. **Serves 4**

Variation
Gouda cheese and ham fondue Prepare as above but add 100 g/4 oz (U.S. ½ cup) chopped cooked ham just before serving.

Rice and Pasta

Because of the time required for rice and pasta to absorb sufficient water for cooking (re-hydration), there is no time advantage to cooking them in the microwave compared to the conventional oven. There are however other advantages – no sticky saucepans, fear of boiling over or steamy kitchens to contend with. Measure the rice or pasta and water into the bowl accurately and leave the microwave to do the rest.

The bonus in preparing rice and pasta however is in the area of reheating. Conventional reheating can overcook rice and pasta making it soft, sticky and tacky. The micro-wave will reheat rice and pasta to freshly-cooked perfection – still firm, separate and full of flavour. It really is worth cooking rice and pasta in bulk for the refrigerator or freezer for good standby emergency meals.

Remember to use a large bowl in which to cook rice and pasta – they can both rehydrate to 2–3 times their original size – and cover with a tight-fitting lid during cooking to keep in the moisture. Observe the standing times too – they will ensure perfect results time and time again.

Guide to cooking rice and pasta

Rice	Quantity	Preparation	Cooking time in minutes on Full power	Standing time
Brown rice	225 g (8 oz)	Place in a deep covered container with 600 ml/1 pint (U.S. 2½ cups) boiling salted water.	20–25	5–10
American easy-cook or pre-cooked rice	225 g (8 oz)	Place in a deep covered container with 600 ml/1 pint (U.S. 2½ cups) boiling salted water.	12	5–10
Long-grain rice	225 g (8 oz)	Place in a deep covered container with 600 ml/1 pint (U.S. 2½ cups) boiling salted water.	10	8–10

Pasta	Quantity	Preparation	Cooking time on Full power in minutes	Standing time
Egg noodles and tagliatelle	225 g (8 oz)	Place in a deep covered container with 600 ml/1 pint (U.S. 2½ cups) boiling salted water and 1 teaspoon oil.	6	5
Macaroni	225 g (8 oz)	Place in a deep covered container with 600 ml/1 pint (U.S. 2½ cups) boiling salted water and 1 teaspoon oil.	10	5
Pasta shells and shapes	225 g (8 oz)	Place in a deep covered container with 900 ml/1½ pints (U.S. 3¾ cups) boiling salted water and 1 teaspoon oil.	12–14	5–10
Spaghetti	225 g (8 oz)	Hold in a deep covered container with 1 litre/1¾ pints (U.S. 4¼ cups) boiling salted water until softened, then submerge or break in half. Add 1 teaspoon oil.	12–14	5–10

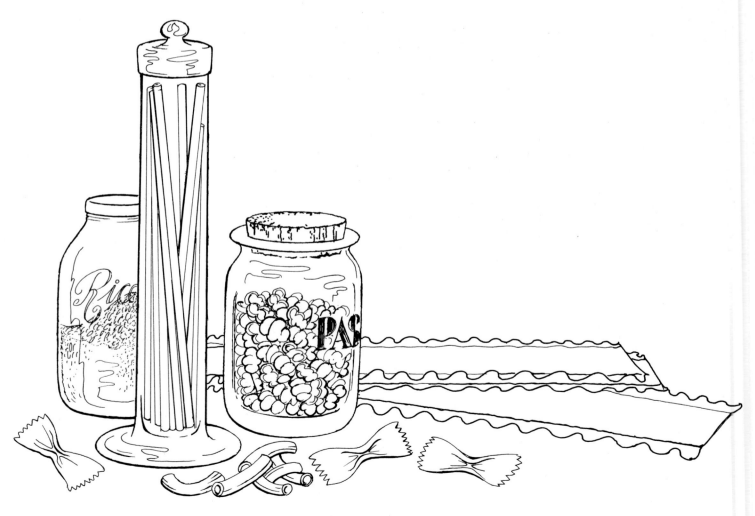

Rice and chicken Taj Mahal

(Illustrated on pages 108–109)

Power setting Full
Total cooking time 12–13 minutes

150 ml/$\frac{1}{4}$ pint (U.S. $\frac{2}{3}$ cup) mayonnaise
1–2 teaspoons curry paste
1 tablespoon mango chutney
salt and freshly ground black pepper
350 g/12 oz (U.S. $\frac{3}{4}$ lb) cooked chicken, cut into bite-sized pieces
175 g/6 oz (U.S. $\frac{3}{4}$ cup) long-grain rice
450 ml/$\frac{3}{4}$ pint (U.S. 2 cups) boiling water
25 g/1 oz (U.S. 2 tablespoons) butter
25 g/1 oz (U.S. $\frac{1}{4}$ cup) whole shelled almonds
$\frac{1}{2}$ small green pepper, seeds removed and chopped
25 g/1 oz (U.S. 2 tablespoons) raisins
3 tablespoons (U.S. $\frac{1}{4}$ cup) French dressing
Garnish
1 sweet red apple, cored and sliced
2 teaspoons lemon juice
watercress sprigs

Mix the mayonnaise with the curry paste to taste, chutney and seasoning to taste. Add the chicken and stir until well coated. Cover and leave to stand for 30 minutes.

Place the rice and water in a deep bowl. Add a little salt, cover and cook for 10 minutes. Allow to stand for 8–10 minutes before draining if necessary. Leave to cool.

Meanwhile place the butter in a small bowl and cook for 1 minute to melt. Add the almonds and cook for 1–2 minutes until golden. Drain on absorbent kitchen towel. Fold the almonds, green pepper, raisins and French dressing into the rice. Season to taste.

Mix the apple slices with the lemon juice to prevent them turning brown. To serve, pile the rice mixture onto a serving dish and top with the curried chicken. Garnish with the apple slices and watercress sprigs. **Serves 4**

Bean and bacon risotto

(Illustrated on pages 108–109)

Power setting Full
Total cooking time 24–26 minutes

225 g/8 oz smoked streaky bacon (U.S. $\frac{1}{2}$ lb smoked bacon slices), rinds removed and chopped
1 onion, peeled and chopped
3 stalks celery, chopped
100 g/4 oz (U.S. $\frac{1}{2}$ cup) long-grain rice
600 ml/1 pint hot chicken stock (U.S. $2\frac{1}{2}$ cups hot chicken bouillon)
salt and freshly ground black pepper
1 (225-g/7.9-oz) can curried beans with sultanas or baked beans in tomato sauce
parsley sprigs to garnish

Place the bacon in a large casserole and cook for 6–8 minutes until browned and crisp. Remove with a slotted spoon and drain on absorbent kitchen towel. Add the onion to the bacon drippings with the celery, cover and cook for 4 minutes. Add the rice, chicken stock and seasoning to taste. Cover and cook for 10 minutes.

Stir in two-thirds of the cooked bacon and the beans, stirring well to blend. Cover and cook for a further 4 minutes. Allow to stand for 5–10 minutes until all the stock has been absorbed by the rice. Serve the risotto topped with the remaining bacon and garnished with the parsley sprigs. **Serves 4**

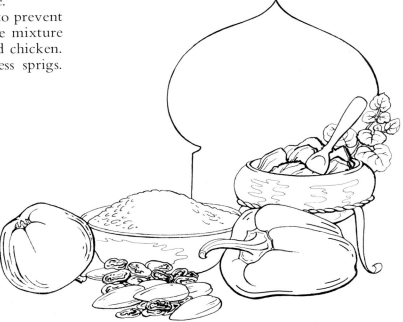

Seaside pasta

Power setting Full
Total cooking time 21–21½ minutes

100 g/4 oz (U.S. ¼ lb) pasta shells
450 ml/¾ pint (U.S. 2 cups) boiling water
1 teaspoon oil
25 g/1 oz (U.S. 2 tablespoons) butter
25 g/1 oz (U.S. ¼ cup) flour
450 ml/¾ pint (U.S. 2 cups) milk
100 g/4 oz (U.S. 1 cup) Edam cheese, grated
1 teaspoon dried mixed herbs
1 (198-g/7-oz) can tuna fish, drained and flaked
tomato slices to garnish

Place the pasta shells in a deep bowl with the water and oil. Cover with cling film, snipping two holes in the top for the steam to escape. Cook for 12 minutes. Allow to stand for 10 minutes then drain.

Place the butter in a large jug and cook for 1 minute to melt. Add the flour and mix well. Gradually add the milk, a little at a time. Cook for 4–4½ minutes, stirring every 1 minute until the sauce is smooth and thickened. Stir in half of the cheese, the herbs and tuna fish. Add the pasta, tossing well to coat. Spoon into a 1-litre/2-pint (U.S. 2½-pint) heatproof dish. Sprinkle with the remaining cheese. Cook for a further 4 minutes until hot and bubbly. Place under a preheated hot grill to brown if liked. Serve hot garnished with tomato slices. **Serves 4**

Ravioli layer bake

Power setting Full
Total cooking time 8 minutes

2 (425-g/15-oz) cans ravioli in tomato sauce
225 g/8 oz (U.S. ½ lb) cheese, sliced
2 teaspoons dried basil or oregano
100 g/4 oz (U.S. 2 cups) potato crisps, crushed

Place two-thirds of one can of ravioli in a deep ovenproof dish. Cover with a third of the cheese. Sprinkle with 1 teaspoon of the basil or oregano. Top with two-thirds of the second can of ravioli and a further third of the cheese. Sprinkle with the remaining basil or oregano and remaining ravioli. Cook for 6 minutes.

Chop the remaining cheese finely and mix with the potato crisps. Spoon on top of the hot ravioli. Cook for a further 2 minutes. Serve hot with a simple mixed salad. **Serves 4**

Tagliatelle al tonno

Power setting Full
Total cooking time 13½–14 minutes

350 g/12 oz (U.S. ¾ lb) tagliatelle
900 ml/1½ pints (U.S. 3¾ cups) boiling water
1 teaspoon oil
1 (198-g/7-oz) can tuna fish
1 onion, peeled and chopped
100 g/4 oz (U.S. 1 cup) mushrooms, sliced
salt and freshly ground black pepper
150 ml/¼ pint double cream (U.S. ⅔ cup heavy cream)

Place the tagliatelle in a deep bowl with the water and oil. Cover with cling film, snipping two holes in the top for the steam to escape. Cook for 8 minutes. Allow to stand for 5 minutes then drain.

Meanwhile, place the oil from the canned tuna in a bowl. Add the onion and cook for 2 minutes. Add the mushrooms, stir to mix and cook for 2 minutes.

Mix the tagliatelle with the flaked tuna fish, onion, mushrooms and seasoning to taste. Pour in the cream and toss to coat. Cook for 1½–2 minutes until hot. Serve at once. **Serves 4**

Tagliatelle country style

Power setting Full
Total cooking time 22–24 minutes

1 tablespoon oil
2 cloves garlic, crushed
1 kg/2 lb tomatoes, peeled and chopped
3 tablespoons (U.S. ¼ cup) chopped parsley
2 tablespoons (U.S. 3 tablespoons) chopped fresh basil
½ teaspoon dried oregano
salt and freshly ground black pepper
350 g/12 oz (U.S. ¾ lb) wholewheat tagliatelle
900 ml/1½ pints (U.S. 3¾ cups) boiling water
1 teaspoon oil
100 g/4 oz (U.S. 1 cup) Cheddar cheese, grated

Place the oil in a bowl with the garlic. Cook for 2 minutes. Remove the garlic with a slotted spoon and discard. Add the tomatoes, parsley, basil, oregano and seasoning to taste. Cook, uncovered, for 8–10 minutes until thick and pulpy.

Place the tagliatelle in a deep bowl with the water and oil. Cover with cling film, snipping two holes in the top for the steam to escape. Cook for 10 minutes. Allow to stand for 10 minutes then drain.

Mix the pasta with the tomato sauce and half of the cheese in a serving dish. Cook for 2 minutes. Serve at once with the remaining cheese sprinkled over. **Serves 6**

Cheese and sweetcorn pasta salad

Power setting Full
Total cooking time 12 minutes

175 g/6 oz (U.S. ⅓ lb) pasta twistetti
450 ml/¾ pint (U.S. 2 cups) boiling water
1 teaspoon oil
175 g/6 oz (U.S. 2 cups) Edam cheese, cubed
1 (340-g/12-oz) can sweetcorn kernels, drained
1 red pepper, seeds removed and chopped
6 tablespoons (U.S. ½ cup) French dressing
1 tablespoon chopped parsley
salt and freshly ground black pepper
3 tomatoes, sliced

Place the pasta in a deep bowl with the water and oil. Cover with cling film, snipping two holes in the top for the steam to escape. Cook for 12 minutes. Allow to stand for 10 minutes then drain and cool.

Mix the pasta with the cheese, sweetcorn, pepper, French dressing, parsley and seasoning to taste. Pile onto a large serving dish and surround with the sliced tomatoes. **Serves 4**

Variations
Cheese and flageolet bean pasta salad Prepare and cook as above but use 1 (340-g/12-oz) can drained flageolet beans instead of the sweetcorn kernels.
Cheese and asparagus pasta salad Prepare and cook as above but use 1 (340-g/12-oz) can drained and chopped asparagus spears instead of the sweetcorn kernels.
Cheese and tuna pasta salad Prepare and cook as above but use 1 (198-g/7-oz) can drained and flaked tuna instead of the sweetcorn kernels.
Cheese and artichoke pasta salad Prepare and cook as above but use 1 (200-g/7-oz) can drained and chopped artichoke hearts in brine instead of the sweetcorn kernels.

Curried chicken pasta salad

Power setting Full
Total cooking time 12 minutes

175 g/6 oz (U.S. ⅓ lb) pasta shells
450 ml/¾ pint (U.S. 2 cups) boiling water
1 teaspoon oil
150 ml/¼ pint (U.S. ⅔ cup) mayonnaise
2 tablespoons single cream (U.S. 3 tablespoons light cream)
2 teaspoons curry powder
225 g/8 oz (U.S. ½ lb) cooked chicken, chopped
2 stalks celery, chopped
1 green pepper, seeds removed and chopped
salt and freshly ground black pepper
lettuce leaves to serve

Place the pasta shells in a deep bowl with the water and oil. Cover with cling film, snipping two holes in the top for the steam to escape. Cook for 12 minutes. Allow to stand for 10 minutes then drain and cool.

Mix the mayonnaise with the cream and curry powder, blending well. Fold in the chicken, pasta shells, celery, pepper and seasoning to taste. Serve on a bed of lettuce leaves. **Serves 4**

Variations
Chilli chicken pasta salad Prepare and cook as above but mix the mayonnaise and cream mixture with 1 teaspoon mild chilli powder and 1 teaspoon chilli relish instead of the curry powder, mixing well.
Curried chicken rice salad Prepare the curried chicken mixture as above without the pasta. Place 100 g/4 oz (U.S. ½ cup) long-grain rice in a deep bowl with 450 ml/¾ pint (U.S. 2 cups) boiling water. Cover and cook for 12 minutes. Allow to stand for 12 minutes, then drain. Allow to cool completely. Fold the cold rice into the curried chicken mixture instead of the pasta to serve.
Curried chicken and almond pasta Prepare and cook as above but add 50 g/2 oz (U.S. ½ cup) blanched slivered almonds to the curried chicken and pasta mixture just before serving.

Spaghetti bolognese

Power setting Full
Total cooking time 37–39 minutes

450 g/1 lb minced beef (U.S. 1 lb ground beef)
1 onion, peeled and chopped
100 g/4 oz (U.S. 1 cup) mushrooms, sliced
15 g/½ oz (U.S. 2 tablespoons) flour
1 (396-g/14-oz) can peeled tomatoes
½ teaspoon dried oregano
2 teaspoons tomato purée (U.S. 2 teaspoons tomato paste)
300 ml/½ pint beef stock (U.S. 1¼ cups beef bouillon)
salt and freshly ground black pepper
450 g/1 lb spaghetti
½ teaspoon oil
1.5 litres/2½ pints (U.S. 6¼ cups) boiling water
15 g/½ oz (U.S. 1 tablespoon) butter

Preheat a large browning dish for 5 minutes. Add the beef and onion, stirring quickly to brown. Cook for 8 minutes, stirring twice during the cooking time. Transfer to a large bowl and stir in the mushrooms and flour. Cook for 1 minute. Add the tomatoes, oregano, tomato purée and stock. Cover and cook for 15 minutes, stirring twice during the cooking time.

Place the spaghetti in a deep bowl with the oil and water. Cook, uncovered, for 8–10 minutes. Cover and leave to stand for 10 minutes.

Return the sauce to the microwave and cook, uncovered, for 5 minutes. Drain the spaghetti and toss in the butter. Place in a heated serving dish and top with the sauce. **Serves 4–6**

Herby sausage lasagne

(Illustrated on pages 108–109)

Power setting Full
Total cooking time 29–31 minutes

350 g/12 oz (U.S. 1½ cups) herb sausagemeat
1 (425-g/15-oz) can peeled tomatoes, chopped
175 g/6 oz tomato purée (U.S. ½ cup tomato paste)
salt and freshly ground black pepper
225 g/8 oz (U.S. ½ lb) lasagne
1 litre/1¾ pints (U.S. 4¼ cups) boiling water
350 g/12 oz (U.S. ¾ lb) Mozzarella cheese, sliced
225 g/8 oz (U.S. 2 cups) cooked sliced mushrooms
25 g/1 oz (U.S. ¼ cup) Parmesan cheese, grated
Garnish
tomato slices
parsley sprigs

Place the sausagemeat in a bowl and cook for 5–6 minutes, stirring every 2 minutes. Add the tomatoes, tomato purée, salt and pepper to taste. Cover and cook for 4 minutes.

Place the lasagne in a deep bowl with the water. Cover with cling film, snipping two holes in the top for the steam to escape. Cook for 6 minutes. Allow to stand for 10 minutes, then drain.

Fill a large dish with alternate layers of lasagne, herby sausage mixture, Mozzarella and mushrooms, finishing with a layer of sausage mixture. Sprinkle with Parmesan cheese and cook for 12 minutes. Garnish with tomato slices and parsley sprigs. **Serves 4–6**

Macaroni vegetable pie

Power setting Full
Total cooking time 34½–37 minutes

450 g/1 lb leeks, sliced
3 stalks celery, sliced
450 ml/¾ pint (U.S. 2 cups) hot milk
salt and freshly ground black pepper
25 g/1 oz (U.S. 2 tablespoons) butter
25 g/1 oz (U.S. ¼ cup) flour
100 g/4 oz (U.S. 1 cup) cheese, grated
100 g/4 oz (U.S. 1 cup) macaroni
300 ml/½ pint (U.S. 1¼ cups) boiling water
1 teaspoon oil
50 g/2 oz (U.S. ½ cup) dried breadcrumbs
Garnish
tomato slices
parsley sprigs

Place the leeks, celery, milk and seasoning to taste in a bowl. Cover and cook for 14 minutes. Strain off the milk and reserve. Place the butter in a jug and cook for 1 minute. Add the flour, mixing well. Gradually add the reserved milk. Cook for 3½–4 minutes, stirring every 1 minute until smooth and thickened. Stir in two-thirds of the cheese.

Place the macaroni in a bowl with the water and oil. Cover with cling film, snipping two holes in the top for the steam to escape. Cook for 10 minutes. Allow to stand for 10 minutes, then drain if necessary. Mix with the cheese sauce. Layer the macaroni mixture with the vegetables in a dish. Mix the breadcrumbs with the remaining cheese and sprinkle over the pie. Cook for 6–8 minutes. Brown under a preheated hot grill if liked. Serve garnished with tomato slices and parsley sprigs. **Serves 2–3**

Savoury cream pasta

Power setting Full
Total cooking time 13–15 minutes

225 g/8 oz (U.S. 2 cups) pasta shells
600 ml/1 pint (U.S. 2½ cups) boiling water
1 teaspoon oil
175 g/6 oz (U.S. 1½ cups) Cheddar cheese, grated
175 g/6 oz (U.S. ¾ cup) cooked ham, shredded
150 ml/¼ pint double cream (U.S. ⅔ cup heavy cream)
salt and freshly ground black pepper
1 tablespoon chopped parsley
black olives (U.S. ripe olives) to garnish (optional)

Place the pasta shells in a deep bowl with the water and oil. Cover with cling film, snipping two holes in the top for the steam to escape. Cook for 10 minutes. Allow to stand for 10 minutes then drain.

Place the cooked pasta in a bowl with the cheese and toss to mix. Add the ham, double cream and seasoning to taste. Cook for 3–5 minutes, stirring every 1 minute until the cheese melts and makes a smooth sauce with the cream. Sprinkle with parsley and garnish with black olives if liked. **Serves 4**

Variations
Savoury cream and tuna pasta Prepare and cook as above but add 1 (198-g/7-oz) can drained and flaked tuna instead of the ham.
Savoury cream and pepper pasta Prepare and cook as above but add 1 (184-g/6½-oz) can drained and chopped pimientos with the ham.
Savoury cream and anchovy pasta Prepare and cook as above but add 1 (50-g/2-oz) can drained and chopped anchovy fillets with the ham.

Lamb, apple and rice salad

Power setting Full
Total cooking time 12 minutes

100 g/4 oz (U.S. $\frac{1}{2}$ cup) long-grain rice
450 ml/$\frac{3}{4}$ pint (U.S. 2 cups) boiling water
1 chicken stock cube (U.S. 1 chicken bouillon cube)
1 large onion, peeled and chopped
4 tablespoons (U.S. $\frac{1}{3}$ cup) mayonnaise
4 teaspoons lemon juice
salt and freshly ground black pepper
350 g/12 oz (U.S. $\frac{3}{4}$ lb) cooked boneless lamb, cubed
2 large sweet apples, cored and sliced
50 g/2 oz (U.S. $\frac{1}{3}$ cup) salted peanuts

Place the rice in a deep bowl with the water and crumbled stock cube. Stir well to mix. Cover and cook for 12 minutes. Allow to stand for 5 minutes, then drain.

Mix the onion into the hot rice and leave to cool.

Meanwhile blend the mayonnaise with the lemon juice and seasoning to taste. Fold into the cooled rice mixture with the lamb, apple and peanuts. Toss well to mix. Serve at once. If you do not wish to serve this salad immediately, add the peanuts just before serving.
Serves 4–6

Variations
Pork, apple and rice salad Prepare and cook as above but use cooked and cubed boneless pork instead of the lamb.
Beef, apple and rice salad Prepare and cook as above but use cooked and cubed boneless beef instead of the lamb and blend the mayonnaise with 1 teaspoon creamed horseradish.
Turkey, apple and rice salad Prepare and cook as above but use cooked and cubed boneless turkey instead of the lamb.

Sauces and Stuffings

A tasty sauce or stuffing can lift an ordinary meal into the luxury class, but they are all too often forgotten because of the time taken to make. A sauce can quickly be pushed to the back of the line of priorities when there is meat, vegetables and other courses to concentrate on.

The microwave should change all that. Sauces can be made in minutes and with the minimum of fuss. No constant stirring for silky smooth results, no burnt saucepan bottoms or lumpy results to contend with. Batch made sauces also seem so convenient when they can be reheated straight from the freezer in 5 minutes.

Stuffings can also be made quickly and the variety is endless. Try experimenting with rice, breadcrumbs or oatmeal for the base and pep up with dried fruits, chopped herbs and spices for interesting results. Cook inside poultry, meat or vegetable dishes, or wrap in cling film to cook and serve separately.

Celery, rice and raisin stuffing

(Illustrated on pages 120–121)

Power setting Full
Total cooking time 5 minutes

25 g/1 oz (U.S. 2 tablespoons) butter
1 small onion, peeled and chopped
2 stalks celery, finely sliced
1 chicken liver, chopped
50 g/2 oz (U.S. ⅓ cup) cooked rice
50 g/2 oz (U.S. ⅓ cup) raisins
salt and freshly ground black pepper
1 egg, beaten

Place the butter in a bowl and cook for 1 minute to melt. Add the onion, celery and liver. Cover and cook for 4 minutes. Add the rice, raisins and seasoning to taste, mixing well. Bind together with the beaten egg. Use as required. **Makes enough to stuff 1 large chicken**

Variations
Liver and sultana stuffing Prepare and cook as above but substitute 175 g/6 oz finely chopped lamb's liver and 175 g/6 oz (U.S. 3 cups) fresh white breadcrumbs.
Herby chestnut stuffing Prepare and cook as above but use 50 g/2 oz (U.S. ½ cup) chopped mushrooms instead of the celery. Cover and cook for just 2 minutes. Use 1 (425-g/15-oz) can unsweetened chestnut purée instead of the rice and 1 teaspoon dried mixed herbs instead of the raisins.

Prune, almond and sausagemeat stuffing

Power setting Full
Total cooking time 3 or 6½–7 minutes

25 g/1 oz (U.S. 2 tablespoons) butter
1 small onion, peeled and chopped
100 g/4 oz (U.S. ⅔ cup) prunes, soaked overnight, stoned and chopped
100 g/4 oz (U.S. ½ cup) pork sausagemeat
50 g/2 oz (U.S. ⅔ cup) rolled oats
50 g/2 oz (U.S. ½ cup) whole shelled almonds, chopped
salt and freshly ground black pepper
1 egg, beaten

Place the butter in a bowl and cook for 1 minute to melt. Add the onion and cook for 2 minutes. Add the prunes, sausagemeat, oats, almonds and seasoning to taste, mixing well. Bind together with some beaten egg.

For individual stuffing balls, divide the mixture into eight portions and roll each into a ball. Place on a roasting rack or plate and cook for 3½–4 minutes, giving the dish a half turn halfway through the cooking time. Allow to stand for 5 minutes before serving. **Makes enough to stuff 1 large chicken or makes 8 stuffing balls**

Lemon, apple and parsley stuffing

Power setting Full
Total cooking time 5 minutes

25 g/1 oz (U.S. 2 tablespoons) butter
1 small onion, peeled and chopped
1 sweet apple, cored and finely chopped
1 chicken liver, chopped
1 tablespoon chopped parsley
grated rind of 1 lemon
50 g/2 oz (U.S. 1 cup) fresh white or brown breadcrumbs
salt and freshly ground black pepper
1 egg, beaten

Place the butter in a bowl and cook for 1 minute to melt. Add the onion, apple and liver. Cover and cook for 4 minutes. Add the parsley, lemon rind, breadcrumbs and seasoning to taste, mixing well. Bind together with some beaten egg. **Makes enough to stuff 1 large chicken**

Bacon and potato stuffing

(Illustrated on pages 120–121)

Power setting Full
Total cooking time 10–12 minutes

225 g/8 oz (U.S. 1⅓ cups) peeled and diced potato
4 tablespoons (U.S. ⅓ cup) water
½ teaspoon salt
25 g/1 oz (U.S. 2 tablespoons) butter
1 onion, peeled and finely chopped
6 rashers streaky bacon (U.S. 6 bacon slices), rinds removed and chopped
½ teaspoon dried tarragon
grated rind and juice of 1 lemon
2 teaspoons Dijon mustard
salt and freshly ground black pepper
1 egg, beaten

Place the potato in a bowl with the water and salt. Cover and cook for 5–7 minutes until just tender. Drain and allow to cool.

Place the butter in a bowl and cook for 1 minute to melt. Add the onion and bacon and cook for 4 minutes. Add the potato, tarragon, lemon rind and juice, mustard and seasoning to taste. Allow to cool.

When cool, bind together with the beaten egg. Use as required. **Makes enough to stuff 1 leg of lamb**

Basic white pouring sauce

Power setting Full
Total cooking time 4½–5 minutes

25 g/1 oz (U.S. 2 tablespoons) butter
25 g/1 oz (U.S. ¼ cup) flour
300 ml/½ pint (U.S. 1¼ cups) milk
salt and freshly ground black pepper

Place the butter in a large jug and cook for 1 minute to melt. Add the flour and mix well to blend. Gradually add the milk and seasoning to taste. Cook for 3½–4 minutes, stirring every 1 minute until the sauce is smooth and thickened. **Makes 300 ml/½ pint (U.S. 1¼ cups)**

Variations

Basic white coating sauce Prepare and cook as above but use 50 g/2 oz (U.S. ¼ cup) butter and 50 g/2 oz (U.S. ½ cup) flour. **Total cooking time 4½–5 minutes**
Mushroom sauce Place 225 g/8 oz (U.S. 2 cups) sliced mushrooms in a bowl with 25 g/1 oz (U.S. 2 tablespoons) butter. Cover and cook for 4 minutes. Gradually add 25 g/1 oz (U.S. ¼ cup) flour and 300 ml/½ pint chicken stock (U.S. 1¼ cups chicken bouillon), 1 teaspoon Worcestershire sauce and a dash of soy sauce. Cook for 3½–4 minutes, stirring every 1 minute. Purée to a smooth sauce if liked. **Total cooking time 7½–8 minutes**
Mustard sauce Prepare and cook as above but add 2 teaspoons dry mustard powder with the flour. **Total cooking time 4½–5 minutes**
Cheese sauce Prepare and cook as above but add 50 g/2 oz (U.S. ½ cup) grated cheese and a pinch of dry mustard powder to the sauce for the last 2 minutes cooking time. **Total cooking time 4½–5 minutes**

Hollandaise sauce

Power setting Full and Medium
Total cooking time 2½ minutes

100 g/4 oz (U.S. ½ cup) butter
2 teaspoons lemon juice
2 teaspoons wine vinegar
½ teaspoon dry mustard powder
2 egg yolks
salt and freshly ground black pepper

Place the butter in a large jug and cook on *Full Power* for 1½ minutes to melt. Mix the lemon juice with the wine vinegar, mustard and egg yolks, and whisk into the butter. Season to taste. Cook on *Medium Power* for 1 minute, stirring after ½ minute. Serve hot with fish or vegetable dishes. **Serves 4**

Quick tomato sauce

Power setting Full
Total cooking time 14 minutes

2 rashers streaky bacon (U.S. 2 bacon slices), rinds removed and chopped
1 large carrot, peeled and sliced
1 stalk celery, sliced
1 large onion, peeled and chopped
1 (398-g/14-oz) can peeled tomatoes
½ teaspoon dried basil
salt and freshly ground black pepper

Place the bacon in a dish and cook for 2 minutes. Add the carrot, celery and onion. Cover and cook for 6 minutes. Add the tomatoes with their juice, the basil and seasoning to taste. Cover and cook for 6 minutes, stirring halfway through the cooking time. Serve chunky or purée in a blender until smooth. **Serves 4**

Apple sauce

Power setting Full
Total cooking time 9 minutes

675 g/1½ lb cooking apples, peeled, cored and sliced
25 g/1 oz (U.S. 2 tablespoons) butter
1½ teaspoons lemon juice
1 tablespoon sugar
1½ tablespoons (U.S. 2 tablespoons) water or apple juice

Place the apples, butter, lemon juice, sugar and water or apple juice in a bowl. Cover and cook for 9 minutes or until the apples are tender.

Serve chunky or purée in a blender until smooth. Serve with meat, poultry, sausages or game. **Makes 450 ml/¾ pint (U.S. 2 cups)**

Bread sauce

Power setting Full
Total cooking time 7 minutes

4 cloves
1 onion, peeled
6 white peppercorns
1 blade mace or pinch of ground nutmeg
½ small bay leaf
300 ml/½ pint (U.S. 1¼ cups) milk
65 g/2½ oz (U.S. 1¼ cups) fresh white breadcrumbs
15 g/½ oz (U.S. 1 tablespoon) butter
2 tablespoons single cream (U.S. 3 tablespoons light cream)
salt and freshly ground black pepper

Press the cloves into the onion and place in a deep bowl with the peppercorns, mace or nutmeg, bay leaf and milk. Cook, uncovered, for 4 minutes.

Strain the milk and add the breadcrumbs. Cook, uncovered, for 2 minutes. Add the butter, cream and seasoning to taste. Cook for 1 minute, stirring halfway through the cooking time. Serve hot with poultry or game. **Makes about 450 ml/¾ pint (U.S. 2 cups)**

Barbecue sauce

Power setting Full
Total cooking time 11 minutes

2 tablespoons (U.S. 3 tablespoons) oil
1 onion, peeled and finely chopped
1 teaspoon dry mustard powder
1 teaspoon malt vinegar
1½ tablespoons (U.S. 2 tablespoons) soy sauce
3 tablespoons tomato purée (U.S. ¼ cup tomato paste)
1½ tablespoons (U.S. 2 tablespoons) lemon juice
40 g/1½ oz (U.S. 3 tablespoons) brown sugar
300 ml/½ pint beef stock (U.S. 1¼ cups beef bouillon)
salt and freshly ground black pepper

Place the oil and onion in a bowl. Cover and cook for 3 minutes. Add the mustard, vinegar, soy sauce, tomato purée, lemon juice, sugar, stock and seasoning to taste, blending well. Cover and cook for 8 minutes, stirring every 2 minutes. Use as a basting sauce or thicken with 2 teaspoons cornflour (U.S. 2 teaspoons cornstarch) for a coating or thicker pouring sauce. **Makes about 450 ml/¾ pint (U.S. 2 cups)**

Gravy

Power setting Full
Total cooking time 5–6 minutes

2 tablespoons (U.S. 3 tablespoons) pan juices or drippings
1–2 tablespoons (U.S. 1–3 tablespoons) flour
300 ml/½ pint hot beef or chicken stock (U.S. 1¼ cups hot beef or chicken bouillon)
salt and freshly ground black pepper

Place the pan juices or drippings in a bowl and stir in sufficient flour, depending on thickness of gravy required. Cook for 3 minutes until the flour turns golden. Gradually add the stock, mixing well. Cook for 2–3 minutes until smooth and boiling. Season to taste and serve. **Makes 300 ml/½ pint (U.S. 1¼ cups)**

Cranberry and orange sauce

Power setting Full
Total cooking time 20 minutes

350 g/12 oz (U.S. 1½ cups) sugar
120 ml/4 fl oz (U.S. ½ cup) water
finely grated rind of 1 orange
450 g/1 lb cranberries

Place the sugar, water, orange rind and cranberries in a large bowl. Cover and cook for 20 minutes, stirring every 5 minutes. Serve hot or cold with poultry or game. **Makes about 900 ml/1½ pints (U.S. 3¾ cups)**

Custard sauce

Power setting Full
Total cooking time 5 minutes

1–2 tablespoons (U.S. 1–3 tablespoons) sugar
2 tablespoons custard powder (U.S. 3 tablespoons
Bird's English dessert mix)
600 ml/1 pint (U.S. 2½ cups) milk

Mix the sugar to taste with the custard powder and a little milk to make a smooth paste. Cook the remaining milk in a jug for 3 minutes. Pour onto the custard powder paste, whisking well. Cook for a further 2 minutes, stirring every ½ minute to keep the sauce smooth. **Makes 600 ml/1 pint (U.S. 2½ cups)**

Variation

Brandy or sherry sauce Prepare and cook as above but use cornflour (U.S. cornstarch) instead of the custard powder and stir 2 tablespoons (U.S. 3 tablespoons) brandy or sweet sherry into the sauce after cooking. **Total cooking time 5 minutes**

Golden syrup sauce

Power setting Full
Total cooking time 3 minutes

2 teaspoons cornflour or arrowroot
(U.S. 2 teaspoons cornstarch or arrowroot powder)
150 ml/¼ pint (U.S. ⅔ cup) water
grated rind and juice of ½ lemon
4 tablespoons golden syrup (U.S. ⅓ cup light corn
syrup)

Mix the cornflour or arrowroot with the water to make a smooth paste. Add the lemon rind and juice and golden syrup, blending well. Cook for 3 minutes, stirring every 1 minute. Serve hot with steamed or baked puddings and as a sauce for ice cream. **Makes 300 ml/½ pint (U.S. 1¼ cups)**

Quick chocolate sauce

Power setting Full
Total cooking time 4–6 minutes

75 g/3 oz (U.S. 6 tablespoons) white sugar
75 g/3 oz (U.S. 6 tablespoons) soft brown sugar
75 g/3 oz cocoa powder (U.S. ¾ cup unsweetened
cocoa)
300 ml/½ pint (U.S. 1¼ cups) milk
1 teaspoon vanilla essence (U.S. 1 teaspoon vanilla
extract)
25 g/1 oz (U.S. 2 tablespoons) butter

Place the sugars, cocoa, milk, vanilla and butter in a bowl, mixing well. Cook for 4–6 minutes, stirring every 1 minute to keep the sauce smooth. When cooked, the sauce will coat the back of a spoon.

Serve warm or cold with ice cream, profiteroles or baked or steamed puddings. **Serves 4–6**

Vegetables and Salads

With the growing list of fresh and frozen vegetables finding their way to our tables, there should be no excuse for vegetable variety. If you choose the variety, the micro-wave will ensure the success — since veget-ables are probably the most successful foods to cook in the microwave. Full firm texture, fresh flavour and strikingly good colours after cooking are all promises made and kept with the microwave.

Cover vegetables tightly during cooking, remembering to prick cling film or polythene bags, if used, to allow steam to escape. Prick the skins of jacket potatoes for the same reason.

Wherever possible cut vegetables into even-sized pieces for cooking or arrange irregular-shaped pieces so that the larger pieces are to the edge of the dish where they will receive the most energy and the thinner ends are to the centre where they will receive less. Observe too a 2–3 minute standing time for the very best results.

Guide to cooking frozen vegetables

Vegetable	Quantity	Amount of water	Time in minutes on Full power
Asparagus	225 g (8 oz)	2 tablespoons (U.S. 3 tablespoons)	6–8
	450 g (1 lb)	4 tablespoons (U.S. ⅓ cup)	11
Broad beans (*U.S. Fava or Lima beans*)	225 g (8 oz)	2 tablespoons (U.S. 3 tablespoons)	8
	450 g (1 lb)	4 tablespoons (U.S. ⅓ cup)	10–11
French or runner beans	225 g (8 oz)	2 tablespoons (U.S. 3 tablespoons)	8
	450 g (1 lb)	4 tablespoons (U.S. ⅓ cup)	10
Broccoli	225 g (8 oz)	2 tablespoons (U.S. 3 tablespoons)	6–8
	450 g (1 lb)	4 tablespoons (U.S. ⅓ cup)	8–10
Brussels sprouts	450 g (1 lb)	4 tablespoons (U.S. ⅓ cup)	13–15
Cabbage	225 g (8 oz)	2 tablespoons (U.S. 3 tablespoons)	6–9
	450 g (1 lb)	4 tablespoons (U.S. ⅓ cup)	10–12
Carrots	225 g (8 oz)	2 tablespoons (U.S. 3 tablespoons)	7–8
	450 g (1 lb)	4 tablespoons (U.S. ⅓ cup)	10
Cauliflower florets	225 g (8 oz)	2 tablespoons (U.S. 3 tablespoons)	5–6
	450 g (1 lb)	4 tablespoons (U.S. ⅓ cup)	8–9
Corn kernels	225 g (8 oz)	2 tablespoons (U.S. 3 tablespoons)	4
	450 g (1 lb)	4 tablespoons (U.S. ⅓ cup)	7–8
Corn on the cob	1 ear		4–6
	2 ears		7–9
Courgettes (*U.S. Zucchini*)	225 g (8 oz)	2 tablespoons (U.S. 3 tablespoons)	4
	450 g (1 lb)	4 tablespoons (U.S. ⅓ cup)	6–7
Mushrooms	225 g (8 oz)	2 tablespoons (U.S. 3 tablespoons)	3–4
Peas	225 g (8 oz)	2 tablespoons (U.S. 3 tablespoons)	4
	450 g (1 lb)	4 tablespoons (U.S. ⅓ cup)	8–9
Chopped or leaf spinach	225 g (8 oz)	2 tablespoons (U.S. 3 tablespoons)	6–7
	450 g (1 lb)	4 tablespoons (U.S. ⅓ cup)	10–11
Mixed root vegetable stewpack	225 g (8 oz)	2 tablespoons (U.S. 3 tablespoons)	7
	450 g (1 lb)	4 tablespoons (U.S. ⅓ cup)	10
Swede (*U.S. Rutabaga*)	225 g (8 oz)	2 tablespoons (U.S. 3 tablespoons)	7
	450 g (1 lb)	4 tablespoons (U.S. ⅓ cup)	11–12
Turnip	225 g (8 oz)	2 tablespoons (U.S. 3 tablespoons)	8
	450 g (1 lb)	4 tablespoons (U.S. ⅓ cup)	12
Diced mixed vegetables	225 g (8 oz)	2 tablespoons (U.S. 3 tablespoons)	5–6
	450 g (1 lb)	4 tablespoons (U.S. ⅓ cup)	4–9

Guide to cooking fresh vegetables

Vegetable	Quantity	Water	Salt	Preparation	Cooking time in minutes on Full power	Instructions
Artichoke – Globe	1	150 ml/¼ pint (U.S. ⅔ cup)	½ teaspoon	Discard tough, outer leaves. Snip tips and cut off stems. Cover to cook. To test if cooked, at minimum time try to pull a leaf from whole artichoke; if it comes away freely, artichoke is cooked.	4–6	Drain upside down before serving.
	2	150 ml/¼ pint (U.S. ⅔ cup)	½ teaspoon		8	
	4	250 ml/8 fl oz (U.S. 1 cup)	1 teaspoon		14–15	
Asparagus	450 g (1 lb)	6 tablespoons (U.S. ½ cup)	½ teaspoon	Place in a dish arranging thicker stems to the outside of the dish and tender tips to the centre. Cover to cook.	12–14	Give the dish a half turn after 6 minutes cooking time.
Beans all except thin French beans	450 g (1 lb)	150 ml/¼ pint (U.S. ⅔ cup)	½ teaspoon	Cover to cook.	14	Stir the beans twice during the cooking time. Test at minimum time if cooked.
French beans	450 g (1 lb)	150 ml/¼ pint (U.S. ⅔ cup)	½ teaspoon	Cover to cook.	5–6	
Broccoli	450 g (1 lb)	150 ml/¼ pint (U.S. ⅔ cup)	½ teaspoon	Place in dish arranging stalks to outside of dish. Cover to cook.	10–12	Stir or give dish a half turn after 6 minutes.
Brussels sprouts	450 g (1 lb)	4 tablespoons (U.S. ⅓ cup)	½ teaspoon	Trim away any damaged leaves. Cut any large sprouts in half. Cover to cook.	8–9	Stir the sprouts after 4 minutes cooking time.

Vegetable	Quantity	Water	Salt	Preparation	Cooking time in minutes on Full power	Instructions
Cabbage						
– shredded	450 g (1 lb)	150 ml/¼ pint (U.S. ⅔ cup)	½ teaspoon	Use a large dish to ensure the cabbage fits loosely. Cover to cook.	8–9	Stir or rearrange halfway through the cooking time.
– wedges	450 g (1 lb)	150 ml/¼ pint (U.S. ⅔ cup)	½ teaspoon		10–12	
Carrots						
– whole	450 g (1 lb)	150 ml/¼ pint (U.S. ⅔ cup)	½ teaspoon	Slice carrots 1 cm/½ inch thick. Diagonally sliced carrots reduce cooking time by 2 minutes. Cover to cook.	12–14	Stir or rearrange halfway through the cooking time.
	1 kg (2 lb)				18–20	
– sliced	450 g (1 lb)	150 ml/¼ pint (U.S. ⅔ cup)	½ teaspoon		12–14	
Cauliflower						
– whole	1 medium about 675 g (1½ lb)	150 ml/¼ pint (U.S. ⅔ cup)	½ teaspoon	Cook whole cauliflower on **Medium/High** power.	14–17	Turn whole cauliflower over halfway through the cooking time. Allow whole cauliflower to stand for 5 minutes before serving. Turn or stir florets halfway through the cooking time.
– florets	450 g (1 lb)	150 ml/¼ pint (U.S. ⅔ cup)	½ teaspoon	Cover to cook.	10–13	
Corn on the cob	1	3 tablespoons (U.S. ½ cup)	–	Cover to cook.	4–6	Cook in husk if liked with no extra water. Rearrange halfway through cooking time if cooking 4–6.
	2	3 tablespoons (U.S. ¼ cup)	–		7–8	
	4	5 tablespoons (U.S. 6 tablespoons	–		14–16	
	6	5 tablespoons (U.S. 6 tablespoons)	–		17–20	
Courgettes (U.S. *zucchini*)						
– sliced	450 g (1 lb)			Cover to cook.	5–6	Dot lightly with 25 g/1 oz (U.S. 2 tablespoons) butter before cooking. Stir or rearrange halfway through the cooking time.
– whole	6 small				7–8	
Leeks						
– sliced	450 g (1 lb)	4 tablespoons (U.S. ⅓ cup)	½ teaspoon	Cover to cook.	10–13	Stir halfway through the cooking time.
Marrow and Pumpkin						
– sliced	450 g (1 lb)			Cover with greaseproof paper to cook.	8–10	Stir halfway through cooking. Add salt after cooking.
Mushrooms						
– whole or sliced	225 g (8 oz)	2 tablespoons (U.S. 3 tablespoons) water or butter		Cover to cook. Add salt, if liked, after cooking.	3–4	Stir halfway through the cooking time.
	450 g (1 lb)				4–6	
Onions						
– whole or quartered	4 medium	4 tablespoons (U.S. ⅓ cup)	½ teaspoon	Cover to cook.	9–11	Stir halfway through the cooking time.
	8 medium				13–15	
Parsnips						
– cubed	450 g (1 lb)	150 ml/¼ pint (U.S. ⅔ cup)	¼ teaspoon	Cover to cook.	8–10	Stir halfway through the cooking time.
Peas						
– shelled	450 g (1 lb)	150 ml/¼ pint (U.S. ⅔ cup)	½ teaspoon	Cover to cook.	9–11	Stir halfway during the cooking time. Add 15–25 g/½–1 oz (1–2 tablespoons) butter after cooking and allow to stand for 5 minutes before serving.
	1 kg (2 lb)	150 ml/¼ pint (U.S. ⅔ cup)	½ teaspoon		12–14	
Potatoes						
– quartered	450 g (1 lb)	150 ml/¼ pint (U.S. ⅔ cup)	½ teaspoon	Cover to cook.	10–14	Stir twice during cooking.
– baked in skins	1			Prick thoroughly and cook on absorbent kitchen towel.	4–6	Potatoes may still feel firm when cooked. Leave to stand 3–4 minutes to soften.
	2				6–8	
	3				8–12	
	4				12–16	
Spinach	450 g (1 lb)			Place in a polythene cookbag and secure loosely with string or an elastic band. Wash but do not dry before cooking.	5–7	Drain before serving. Add salt after cooking.
Tomatoes						
– halved	2			Add a knob of butter and a little salt and pepper to each half before cooking. Cover to cook.	1–1½	
Turnips and Swede (U.S. *rutabaga*) – cubed	450 g (1 lb)	150 ml/¼ pint (U.S. ⅔ cup)	¼ teaspoon	Cover to cook.	12–14	Stir twice during the cooking time.

Tasty bacon potatoes

Power setting Full
Total cooking time 24–29 minutes

4 large potatoes, scrubbed
225 g/8 oz rashers streaky bacon (U.S. ½ lb bacon
slices), rinds removed
4 tablespoons (U.S. ⅓ cup) milk
salt and freshly ground black pepper
4 rashers streaky bacon (U.S. 4 bacon slices), rinds
removed
4 tablespoons soured cream (U.S. ⅓ cup dairy sour
cream) (optional)
snipped chives to garnish (optional)

Prick the potatoes thoroughly and place on absorbent
kitchen towel. Cook for 12–16 minutes until cooked.
Leave to stand while preparing the bacon.

Place the 225 g/8 oz bacon on a plate or roasting rack
and cover with absorbent kitchen towel. Cook for 6½–7
minutes, turning the rashers over halfway through the
cooking time. Chop coarsely.

Slice the tops off the potatoes and scoop out the soft
potato into a bowl. Mix with the chopped bacon, milk
and seasoning to taste. Pile back into the skins. Cook for
2 minutes to reheat.

Meanwhile, pleat the 4 bacon rashers and push onto a
wooden skewer. Cook for 3½–4 minutes until crisp.

Top each potato with a spoonful of soured cream,
sprinkling of chives if liked, and a pleated bacon rasher.
Serves 4

Green beans provençal

Power setting Full
Total cooking time 20½–22 minutes

1 onion, peeled and chopped
1½ tablespoons (U.S. 2 tablespoons) oil
1 clove garlic, peeled and crushed
1 (425-g/15-oz) can peeled tomatoes
1 (141-g/5-oz) can tomato purée (U.S. tomato paste)
4 tablespoons red wine, beef stock or tomato juice
(U.S. ⅓ cup red wine, beef bouillon or tomato juice)
1 tablespoon brown sugar
1 teaspoon Worcestershire sauce
½ teaspoon dried oregano
½ teaspoon dried basil
½ teaspoon salt
¼ teaspoon freshly ground black pepper
450 g/1 lb runner beans (U.S. 1 lb green beans), sliced
150 ml/¼ pint (U.S. ⅔ cup) water

Place the onion, oil and garlic in a large bowl. Cook for
1½–2 minutes. Add the tomatoes with their juice,
tomato purée, red wine, beef stock or tomato juice,
sugar, Worcestershire sauce, oregano, basil, half the salt
and the pepper, mixing well. Cover and cook for 6–7
minutes, stirring halfway through the cooking time.
Allow to stand while preparing the beans.

Place the beans in a bowl with the water and
remaining salt. Cover and cook for 10 minutes. Drain
and place in a serving dish. Top with the tomato sauce,
cover and cook for 3 minutes. Serve hot. **Serves 4**

Western baked onions

Power setting Full
Total cooking time 16–19 minutes

4 large onions, peeled
4 tablespoons (u.s. ⅓ cup) water
½ teaspoon salt
100 g/4 oz rashers streaky bacon (u.s. ¼ lb bacon slices), chopped
1 (225-g/7.9-oz) can curried baked beans with sultanas
2 tablespoons (u.s. 3 tablespoons) chutney

Place the onions in a shallow dish with the water and salt. Cover and cook for 8–10 minutes until just tender. Drain and cool.

Remove the centre of each onion with a teaspoon and roughly chop. Place the chopped onion in a bowl with the bacon. Cook for 5 minutes. Stir in the curried beans with sultanas and chutney. Spoon the bean mixture into the cavity of each onion. Place in a dish and cook for 3–4 minutes until hot and bubbly. **Serves 4**

Colcannon

Power setting Full
Total cooking time 28–30 minutes

1 kg/2 lb potatoes, peeled and quartered
300 ml/½ pint (u.s. 1¼ cups) water
1 teaspoon salt
75 g/3 oz (u.s. 6 tablespoons) butter
2 tablespoons (u.s. 3 tablespoons) milk
450 g/1 lb (u.s. 6 cups) kale or green cabbage, shredded
150 ml/¼ pint chicken stock (u.s. ⅔ cup chicken bouillon)
salt and freshly ground black pepper
ground mace

Place the potatoes in a bowl with the water and salt. Cover and cook for 18–20 minutes, stirring twice during the cooking time. Drain and mash with 25 g/1 oz (u.s. 2 tablespoons) of the butter and the milk.

Meanwhile, place the cabbage in a bowl with the stock. Cover and cook for 8 minutes. Drain well.

Mix the potato with the cabbage and salt, pepper and mace to taste. Cook for 2 minutes to reheat. Make a hollow in the middle and put in the rest of the butter so that it melts as the dish is served. **Serves 6**

Bean and bacon savoury

Power setting Full
Total cooking time 20–22 minutes

25 g/1 oz (U.S. 2 tablespoons) butter
1 small onion, peeled and chopped
5 rashers back bacon (U.S. 5 slices Canadian bacon),
rinds removed
450 g/1 lb broad beans (U.S. 1 lb fava or lima beans)
300 ml/½ pint light stock (U.S. 1¼ cups light bouillon)
chopped parsley to garnish

Place the butter in a bowl and cook for 1 minute to melt.
Add the onion and bacon. Cook for 5 minutes. Add the
beans and stock, stirring well to mix. Cover and cook
for 14–16 minutes, stirring twice during the cooking
time. Serve garnished with chopped parsley. **Serves 4**

Variations

French bean and bacon savoury Prepare and cook
as above but use 450 g/1 lb French beans instead of the
broad beans. Cover and cook for 8–9 minutes. **Total
cooking time 14–15 minutes**

Broccoli and bacon savoury Prepare and cook as
above but use 450 g/1 lb broccoli spears instead of the
broad beans.

Celery and bacon savoury Prepare and cook as
above but use 450 g/1 lb chopped celery stalks instead of
the broad beans. After adding the celery and stock,
cover and cook for 16–18 minutes. **Total cooking time
22–24 minutes**

Corn and parsley redskins

**Power setting Full or Full and Medium
Total cooking time 7 or 10½ minutes**

8 medium-sized tomatoes
25 g/1 oz (U.S. 2 tablespoons) butter
1 onion, peeled and chopped
1 (198-g/7-oz) can sweetcorn kernels, drained
100 g/4 oz (U.S. 2 cups) fresh white breadcrumbs
2 tablespoons chopped parsley
salt and freshly ground black pepper

Cut the tops off the tomatoes from the stem end and reserve. Scoop out the seeds and discard.

Place the butter in a bowl and cook on *Full Power* for 1 minute to melt. Add the onion and cook on *Full Power* for 2 minutes. Add the corn, breadcrumbs, parsley and seasoning to taste. Spoon equal amounts into the tomato cases and top with the reserved lids.

Place on a plate and cook on *Full Power* for 4 minutes or on *Medium Power* for 7½ minutes, giving the dish a half turn once during the cooking. Serve hot garnished with parsley sprigs. **Serves 4**

Variations
Corn and celery redskins Prepare and cook as above but add 2 stalks chopped celery instead of the parsley.
Corn and mushroom redskins Prepare and cook as above but add 50 g/2 oz (U.S. ½ cup) sliced mushrooms to the corn mixture.
Pepper, corn and parsley redskins Prepare and cook as above but use a drained 326-g/11½-oz can sweetcorn with peppers instead of corn kernels and omit the onion.
Bean and parsley redskins Prepare and cook as above but use a drained 213-g/7½-oz can butter beans instead of the corn kernels.
Corn, bacon and parsley redskins Prepare and cook as above but add 2 cooked and chopped rashers of streaky bacon (U.S. 2 cooked and chopped bacon slices) to the corn mixture. Cook the bacon on a plate for 1–2 minutes until cooked and browned. **Total cooking time 8–9 or 11½–12½ minutes**

Ratatouille

Power setting Full
Total cooking time 30–32 minutes

4 tablespoons (U.S. $\frac{1}{3}$ cup) oil
2 onions, peeled and chopped
2 cloves garlic, crushed
2 green peppers, seeds removed and sliced
2 red peppers, seeds removed and sliced
350 g/12 oz courgettes (U.S. $\frac{3}{4}$ lb zucchini), sliced
350 g/12 oz aubergine (U.S. $\frac{3}{4}$ lb eggplant), sliced
450 g/1 lb tomatoes, peeled, seeds removed and chopped
salt and freshly ground black pepper

Place the oil, onions, garlic and peppers in a large dish. Cover and cook for 7 minutes, stirring halfway through the cooking time. Add the courgettes and aubergine, stirring well. Cover and cook for 15 minutes. Add the tomatoes and seasoning to taste. Cover and cook for 8–10 minutes until cooked and reduced to a thick pulpy mixture. Allow to stand, covered, for 5 minutes before serving. **Serves 4–6**

Storecupboard vegetable slice

Power setting Full
Total cooking time 9–10 minutes

2 tablespoons (U.S. 3 tablespoons) dried onions
120 ml/4 fl oz (U.S. $\frac{1}{2}$ cup) tomato juice
3 (213-g/7.5-oz) cans red kidney beans
3 (396-g/14-oz) cans cannellini beans
1 (227-g/8-oz) packet frozen broad beans (U.S. 8-oz packet frozen fava or lima beans), thawed and drained
50 g/2 oz (U.S. $\frac{1}{2}$ cup) mushrooms, sliced
200 g/7 oz (U.S. 1 cup) celery, chopped
3 tablespoons (U.S. $\frac{1}{4}$ cup) natural bran
1 tablespoon soy sauce
1 tablespoon oil
2 eggs, beaten
salt and freshly ground black pepper

Place the onion in a bowl with the tomato juice. Cover and cook for 2 minutes. Chop or mash the drained kidney and cannellini beans together. Add the broad beans, onion and tomato mixture, mushrooms, celery and bran. Beat the soy sauce with the oil and egg, and mix into the bean mixture. Season to taste and pack into a 1-kg/2-lb greased loaf dish. Cook for 5 minutes, wrap in foil and leave to stand for 5 minutes. Remove the foil and cook for a further 2–3 minutes. Cool under a weight and serve sliced. **Serves 8**

Ham and avocado salad

Power setting Medium
Total cooking time 11–12 minutes

1 (450-g/1-lb) joint collar ham or bacon (U.S. 1-lb
smoked shoulder butt)
2 avocados, peeled, stoned and sliced
2 large oranges, peeled, pith removed and segmented
6 tablespoons (U.S. ½ cup) French dressing
1 clove garlic, crushed
salt and freshly ground black pepper
1 lettuce, shredded
mustard and cress to garnish

Place the ham or bacon joint in a roasting bag and secure
the end loosely with string or an elastic band. Cook for
11–12 minutes, turning halfway during the cooking
time. Allow to cool.

Chop the ham into bite-sized pieces. Place in a bowl
with the avocado slices, orange segments, French
dressing, garlic, seasoning to taste and lettuce. Toss
gently to mix.

Chill lightly before serving garnished with mustard
and cress. **Serves 4**

Summer brisket salad

Power setting Full
Total cooking time 12 minutes

175 g/6 oz (U.S. 1½ cups) pasta shells
450 ml/¾ pint (U.S. 2 cups) boiling water
1 teaspoon oil
225 g/8 oz cooked salt beef brisket, chopped (U.S. 1½
cups cooked diced corned beef brisket)
6 spring onions (U.S. 6 scallions), sliced
175 g/6 oz black grapes (U.S. ⅓ lb purple grapes),
halved and pips removed
1 (5–7.5-cm/2–3-inch) piece cucumber, chopped
4 tablespoons (U.S. ⅓ cup) French dressing
½ teaspoon dried basil
salt and freshly ground black pepper
lettuce leaves to serve

Place the pasta shells in a deep bowl with the water and
oil. Cover with cling film, snipping two holes in the top
for the steam to escape. Cook for 12 minutes. Allow to
stand for 10 minutes, then drain and cool.

Mix the pasta with the beef, spring onions, grapes,
cucumber, French dressing, basil and seasoning to taste.
Toss well to coat. Serve on a bed of lettuce leaves.
Serves 4

Spicy tomato cocktail

Power setting Full
Total cooking time 4 minutes

1 tablespoon oil
2 large onions, peeled and chopped
1.15 litres/2 pints (U.S. 2½ pints) tomato juice
½ teaspoon dried thyme
1 tablespoon Worcestershire sauce
salt and freshly ground black pepper
4 stalks celery, finely chopped
1 green pepper, seeds removed and chopped
1 red pepper, seeds removed and chopped
1 small cucumber, finely chopped
2 tablespoons chopped watercress

Place the oil in a bowl with one of the onions. Cook for 4 minutes until soft. Add to the tomato juice with the thyme, Worcestershire sauce and seasoning to taste. Purée until smooth in a blender.

Add the celery, peppers, cucumber, remaining onion and watercress.

Chill thoroughly before serving. **Serves 4**

Variations

Spicy vegetable cocktail Prepare and cook as above but use 1.15 litres/2 pints (U.S. 2½ pints) canned or bottled vegetable juice drink instead of the tomato juice.

Spicy carrot juice cocktail Prepare and cook as above but use 1.15 litres/2 pints (U.S. 2½ pints) canned or bottled carrot juice instead of the tomato juice.

Spicy mint and tomato cocktail Prepare and cook as above but use 2 teaspoons chopped fresh mint instead of the dried thyme and garnish with fresh mint leaves instead of the chopped watercress leaves.

Corn coleslaw with peanut dressing

Power setting Full
Total cooking time 1–1½ minutes

1 (340-g/12-oz) can sweetcorn kernels with peppers
225 g/8 oz (U.S. 3 cups) cabbage, finely shredded
2 carrots, peeled and grated
1 sweet apple, cored and chopped
50 g/2 oz (U.S. ⅓ cup) raisins
Dressing
3 tablespoons (U.S. ¼ cup) crunchy peanut butter
150 ml/¼ pint soured cream (U.S. ⅔ cup dairy sour cream)
2 tablespoons (U.S. 3 tablespoons) lemon juice
salt and freshly ground black pepper
lettuce leaves to serve
watercress sprigs to garnish

Drain the sweetcorn reserving the can juice. Mix the corn with the cabbage, carrots, apple and raisins.

For the dressing, place the reserved can juice in a bowl with the peanut butter, soured cream, lemon juice and seasoning to taste. Mix well and cook for 1–1½ minutes until hot but not boiling. Pour over the coleslaw mixture and toss to coat. Allow to cool.

Serve the coleslaw on a bed of lettuce garnished with watercress sprigs. **Serves 4–6**

Variations
Cheese and corn coleslaw with peanut dressing Prepare and cook as above but add 100 g/4 oz (U.S. 1 cup) grated cheese to the cooled coleslaw. Toss to mix before serving on a bed of lettuce.
Fruit and corn coleslaw with peanut dressing Prepare and cook as above but add 100 g/4 oz (U.S. ¼ lb) halved seedless grapes to the coleslaw before adding the dressing. Toss well to mix.
Corn and orange coleslaw with peanut dressing Prepare and cook as above but add the chopped flesh from 1 orange to the coleslaw before adding the dressing. Toss well to mix. Substitute orange juice for lemon juice in the dressing if liked.
Pineapple and corn coleslaw with peanut dressing Prepare and cook as above but add the chopped flesh of 1 small pineapple to the coleslaw before adding the dressing.
Corn coleslaw with peanut yogurt dressing Prepare and cook as above but use 150 ml/¼ pint natural yogurt instead of the soured cream.

Bread, Cakes and Biscuits

This is probably the most controversial area of microwave cooking – and why? Simply because the microwave does not cook to a golden brown our favourite tea time specialities – breads, pastries, cakes and biscuits. A frosting, icing or colourful, crunchy topping will disguise this lack of surface browning – see pages 18–19 for more suggestions.

Microwave cooking of such dishes also means that you cannot use your traditional metal bakeware. You can however use special microwave bakeware available now in most popular sizes and shapes or improvise with soufflé dishes and paper boxes for the same results.

Even if you decide this is the one area where you will cook conventionally then use your microwave to help. It will efficiently soften butter for creaming purposes, melt chocolate for spreading, encourage proving of bread dough in extra quick times and toast nuts and coconut with little effort.

Basic white bread

(Illustrated on pages 142–143)

Power setting Full and Low

1 teaspoon sugar
2 teaspoons dried yeast (U.S. 2 teaspoons active dry yeast)
450 ml/¾ pint (U.S. 2 cups) warm water
675 g/1½ lb strong plain bread flour (U.S. 6 cups all-purpose bread flour)
2 teaspoons salt
15 g/½ oz lard (U.S. 1 tablespoon shortening)
2 teaspoons oil
poppy seeds, cracked wheat, crushed cornflakes, oatmeal, sesame seeds, caraway seeds, chopped nuts etc. to sprinkle

Mix the sugar with the yeast and half of the water. Leave to stand until well risen and frothy, about 10 minutes.

Sift the flour with the salt into a mixing bowl and cook on *Full Power* for ½ minute until warm. Rub in the lard. Add the yeast liquid and remaining water, and mix to a pliable dough. Knead on a lightly floured surface until smooth and elastic, about 5–10 minutes. Return to the bowl, cover with cling film and leave in a warm place until doubled in size. You can hasten this process by cooking occasionally on *Full Power* for 5 seconds.

Knead the dough for a further 2–3 minutes then shape as required. **Makes 1 (900-g/2-lb) loaf, 1 cottage loaf, 1 plait, 1 crown loaf, 1 cob or 16–18 shaped rolls**

To make a cottage loaf Divide the dough into two pieces of ⅓ and ⅔. Knock back and knead each piece until firm. Using the palm of the hand, shape the larger piece into a round and place on a lightly greased tray or large plate. Similarly shape the small piece and place on top of the larger round. Using the floured handle of a wooden spoon, pierce through the centre of the two rounds, joining them together. Cover loosely with cling film and prove until doubled in size as before. Brush with the oil and sprinkle with the chosen topping if used. Cook on *Full Power* for 5 minutes, giving the dish a half turn twice during the cooking time *or* cook on *Full Power* for 1 minute then on *Low Power* for 7–9 minutes, giving the dish a half turn three times during the cooking time. Leave to stand for 10 minutes, then transfer to a wire rack to cool. If a brown crust is liked, place the loaf under a preheated hot grill until golden. **Total cooking time 5½ or 7½–9½ minutes**

To make a cob Using the palm of the hand, shape the dough into a round. Score the top into four sections with a sharp knife. Place on a lightly greased tray or large plate. Cover loosely with cling film and prove until doubled in size as before. Brush with the oil and sprinkle with the chosen topping if used. Cook on *Full Power* for 5 minutes, giving the dish a half turn twice

during the cooking time *or* cook on *Full Power* for 1 minute then on *Low Power* for 7–9 minutes, giving the dish a half turn three times during the cooking time. Leave to stand for 10 minutes, then transfer to a wire rack to cool. If a brown crust is liked, place the loaf under a preheated hot grill until golden. **Total cooking time 5½ or 7½–9½ minutes**

To make a crown Divide the dough into eight equal-sized pieces. Roll each into a ball with the palm of the hand. Place seven of the balls in a circle in a 18-cm/7-inch glass flan dish and one in the centre. Cover loosely with cling film and prove until doubled in size as before. Brush with the oil and sprinkle with the chosen topping if used. Cook on *Full Power* for 5 minutes, giving the dish a half turn twice during the cooking time *or* cook on *Full Power* for 1 minute then on *Low Power* for 7–9 minutes, giving the dish a half turn three times during the cooking time. Leave to stand for 10 minutes, then

transfer to a wire rack to cool. If a brown crust is liked, place the loaf under a preheated hot grill until golden. **Total cooking time 5$\frac{1}{2}$ or 7$\frac{1}{2}$–9$\frac{1}{2}$ minutes**

To make a plait Divide the dough into three equal-sized pieces. Using the hands, roll each piece into a strip about 35 cm/14 inches long. Gather the ends together and plait. Gently press together at each end to seal. Place on a lightly greased tray or large plate. Cover loosely with cling film and prove until doubled in size as before. Brush with the oil and sprinkle with the chosen topping if used. Cook on *Full Power* for 5 minutes, giving the dish a half turn twice during the cooking time *or* cook on *Full Power* for 1 minute then on *Low Power* for 7–9 minutes, giving the dish a half turn three times during the cooking time. Leave to stand foR 10 minutes, then transfer to a wire rack to cool. If a brown crust is liked, place the loaf under a preheated hot grill until golden. **Total cooking time 5$\frac{1}{2}$ or 7$\frac{1}{2}$–9$\frac{1}{2}$ minutes**

To make rolls Divide the dough into 16–18 pieces and shape into clover leafs, coils, knots, rounds, baps or s-shapes. Place on two lightly greased trays or large plates. Cover loosely with cling film and prove until doubled in size as before. Brush with the oil and sprinkle with the chosen topping if used. Cook in two batches on *Full Power* for 2 minutes, rearranging halfway through the cooking time. Cook the second batch in the same way. If a brown crust is liked, place the rolls under a preheated hot grill until golden. **Total cooking time 4$\frac{1}{2}$ minutes**

Variation
Wheatmeal and wholemeal bread Prepare and cook as above but use 4 teaspoons dried yeast (U.S. 4 teaspoons active dry yeast) for both wheatmeal and wholemeal flours. For wholemeal bread also increase the quantity of water to 500 ml/17 fl oz (U.S. generous 1 pint).

Orange pork rolls

Power setting Full
Total cooking time 15 minutes

4 round crusty bread rolls
2 tablespoons (U.S. 3 tablespoons) oil
1 onion, peeled and finely chopped
1 clove garlic, crushed
450 g/1 lb minced pork (U.S. 1 lb ground pork)
2 teaspoons Meaux mustard
1 teaspoon dried sage
finely grated rind and juice of 1 orange
salt and freshly ground black pepper
watercress sprigs to garnish

Cut a circle around the top of each roll with a sharp knife and remove the 'lid'. Scoop out the soft bread and make into crumbs.

Place the oil in a large bowl. Add the onion and garlic. Cover and cook for 3 minutes. Add the pork and cook for 8 minutes, stirring two or three times during the cooking time. Add the breadcrumbs, mustard, sage, orange rind and juice and seasoning to taste.

Spoon the pork filling into the bread cases and top with the lids. Place on absorbent kitchen towel and cook for 4 minutes until hot. Garnish with watercress sprigs and serve with a little mixed salad. **Serves 4**

Crunchy oat florentines

(Illustrated on pages 142–143)

Power setting Full and Medium/High
Total cooking time $9\frac{1}{2}$–$10\frac{1}{2}$ minutes

75 g/3 oz (U.S. 6 tablespoons) butter
3 tablespoons golden syrup (U.S. $\frac{1}{4}$ cup light corn syrup)
100 g/4 oz (U.S. $1\frac{1}{4}$ cups) rolled oats
25 g/1 oz soft brown sugar (U.S. 2 tablespoons light brown sugar)
25 g/1 oz (U.S. 3 tablespoons) chopped mixed candied peel
25 g/1 oz glacé cherries (U.S. 3 tablespoons candied cherries), coarsely chopped
25 g/1 oz (U.S. $\frac{1}{4}$ cup) hazelnuts, coarsely chopped
100 g/4 oz plain chocolate (U.S. $\frac{2}{3}$ cup semi-sweet chocolate pieces)

Place the butter and golden syrup in a bowl and cook on *Full Power* for $1\frac{1}{2}$ minutes to melt. Stir well. Add the oats, sugar, peel, cherries and hazelnuts, mixing well to blend.

Lightly grease a 20-cm/8-inch square dish and line the base with a sheet of rice paper.

Spoon the mixture into the dish and level the surface with the back of a spoon. Cook on *Medium/High Power* for 6 minutes, giving the dish a half turn every 2 minutes. Allow to cool slightly, then cut into 16 finger biscuits and place on a wire rack to cool.

Place the chocolate in a bowl and cook on *Full Power* for 2–3 minutes to melt, stirring halfway through the cooking time. Spread over the tops of the florentines and mark into a zig-zag pattern with the prongs of a fork. Leave to set. **Makes 16**

Strawberry shortcake

(Illustrated on pages 142–143)

Power setting Defrost
Total cooking time 16 minutes

Shortcake
450 g/1 lb plain flour (U.S. 4 cups all-purpose flour)
100 g/4 oz icing sugar (U.S. 1 cup confectioners' sugar)
275 g/10 oz (U.S. $1\frac{1}{4}$ cups) unsalted butter, softened
4 tablespoons (U.S. $\frac{1}{3}$ cup) chopped nuts
Filling
450 g/1 lb (U.S. 3 cups) strawberries, hulled
2 tablespoons (U.S. 3 tablespoons) red wine, orange juice or brandy
2 tablespoons (U.S. 3 tablespoons) sugar
450 ml/$\frac{3}{4}$ pint double cream (U.S. 2 cups heavy cream)

Sift the flour and icing sugar into a bowl. Rub in the butter until the mixture resembles fine breadcrumbs. Line the bases of two (23-cm/9-inch) shallow dishes with greaseproof paper. Divide the shortcake mixture between the prepared dishes, smoothing the surface level with the back of a spoon. Sprinkle evenly with the nuts and cook separately on *Defrost Power* for 8 minutes, giving the dish a quarter turn every 2 minutes, or until a skewer inserted into the centre of the shortcake comes out clean. Leave to cool in the dish for at least 1 hour. Cook the second shortcake in the same way.

Meanwhile for the filling, slice three-quarters of the strawberries and place in a dish with the red wine, orange juice or brandy and sugar. Leave to marinate for 1 hour.

Place one of the shortcake rounds onto a serving dish, removing any greaseproof paper. Whip two-thirds of the cream until it stands in soft peaks and fold in the marinated strawberry mixture. Spoon on top of the shortcake base. Top with the second shortcake round, removing any greaseproof paper. Whip the remaining cream until it stands in soft peaks. Place in a piping bag fitted with a large star nozzle and pipe swirls of cream on top of the shortcake. Decorate with the remaining whole strawberries. Best eaten on the day of making. **Serves 6**

Speedy soda bread

Power setting Full and Medium
Total cooking time 8 minutes

450 g/1 lb plain wholemeal flour (U.S. 4 cups
wholewheat flour)
2 teaspoons bicarbonate of soda (U.S. 2 teaspoons
baking soda)
2 teaspoons cream of tartar
1 teaspoon salt
25 g/1 oz lard (U.S. 2 tablespoons shortening)
2 teaspoons sugar
300 ml/½ pint (U.S. 1¼ cups) milk
1 tablespoon lemon juice
25 g/1 oz (U.S. ⅓ cup) rolled oats

Sift the flour with the bicarbonate of soda, cream of
tartar and salt. Rub in the lard until the mixture
resembles fine breadcrumbs. Fold in the sugar, mixing
well. Mix the milk with the lemon juice and add to the
flour mixture binding well to make a soft dough. Knead
lightly and shape into a round. Place on a greased plate
and mark into four sections with a sharp knife. Sprinkle
with the oats.

Cook on *Medium Power* for 5 minutes, give the dish a
half turn and cook on *Full Power* for a further 3 minutes.
Allow to stand for 10 minutes, then transfer to a wire
rack to cool. Best eaten on day of making. **Makes 1 loaf**

Savoury peanut bread

Power setting Full
Total cooking time 8–9 minutes

300 ml/½ pint (U.S. 1¼ cups) milk
4 tablespoons (U.S. ⅓ cup) smooth peanut butter
100 g/4 oz soft brown sugar (U.S. ⅔ cup light brown
sugar)
450 g/1 lb plain flour (U.S. 4 cups all-purpose flour)
1 tablespoon baking powder
100 g/4 oz (U.S. ½ cup) unsalted butter
1 egg, beaten
100 g/4 oz (U.S. ⅔ cup) salted peanuts, chopped
Topping
1½ tablespoons (U.S. 2 tablespoons) salted peanuts
50 g/2 oz (U.S. ½ cup) Gouda cheese, grated

Place the milk in a jug with the peanut butter and sugar.
Cook for 3 minutes until melted and dissolved. Cool.

Sift the flour with the baking powder. Rub in the
butter until the mixture resembles fine breadcrumbs.
Add the cooled milk mixture, egg and chopped
peanuts. Mix well. Grease a 900-g/2-lb glass loaf dish
and line the base with greaseproof paper. Spoon the
mixture into the dish. Smooth the top. Sprinkle with
the whole peanuts and grated cheese. Cook for 5–5
minutes, giving the dish a half turn halfway through the
cooking time.

Allow to stand for 10 minutes, then turn out onto a
wire rack to cool. Serve sliced and buttered. **Makes 1
(900-g/2-lb) loaf**

Chocolate cherry cakes

Power setting Full
Total cooking time 4 minutes

50 g/2 oz (U.S. ¼ cup) butter
50 g/2 oz (U.S. ¼ cup) sugar
1 egg, beaten
50 g/2 oz self-raising flour (U.S. ½ cup all-purpose
flour sifted with ½ teaspoon baking powder)
1 tablespoon cocoa powder (U.S. 1 tablespoon
unsweetened cocoa)
1 tablespoon golden syrup (U.S. 1 tablespoon light
corn syrup)
4–6 teaspoons milk
Decoration
150 ml/¼ pint double cream (U.S. ⅔ cup heavy
cream), whipped
maraschino cherries, grated chocolate

Cream the butter with the sugar until light and fluffy. Beat in the egg, mixing well. Sift the flour with the cocoa powder and fold into the creamed mixture with golden syrup and milk until soft, almost runny.

Place six double-thickness paper bun cases in a microwave muffin pan or in six small cups. Using half the cake mixture, half-fill the cake cases with the chocolate mixture. Cook for 2 minutes, giving the dish a half turn after 1 minute. Place on a wire rack to cool. Repeat with the remaining mixture.

When cool, top each cake with a swirl of cream, a cherry and a little grated chocolate. **Makes 12**

Jam and cream sponge

Power setting Full
Total cooking time 6½–7½ minutes

Cake
175 g/6 oz (U.S. ¾ cup) butter or margarine
175 g/6 oz (U.S. ¾ cup) sugar
3 eggs, beaten
175 g/6 oz plain flour (U.S. 1½ cups all-purpose flour)
pinch of salt, 2 teaspoons baking powder
2 tablespoons (U.S. 3 tablespoons) hot water
Filling
150 ml/¼ pint double cream (U.S. ⅔ cup heavy
cream), whipped
5 tablespoons (U.S. 6 tablespoons) strawberry jam

Cream the butter with the sugar until light and fluffy. Beat in the egg, mixing well. Sift the flour with the salt and baking powder and fold in with the water.

Line a 20-cm/8-inch cake dish or soufflé dish with cling film or lightly grease and line the base with greaseproof paper. Spoon the cake mixture into the prepared dish and cook for 6½–7½ minutes, giving the dish a half turn every 2 minutes to ensure even cooking and rising. The cake will still be slightly moist on top when cooked but will dry with the residual heat in the cake upon standing. Allow to stand for 5 minutes, then turn out onto a wire rack to cool.

When cold, split the cake in half horizontally. Sandwich together with the cream and jam. Dust the top with icing sugar before serving. **Serves 6**

Ginger lemon cake

Power setting Full
Total cooking time 6 minutes

Cake
50 g/2 oz (U.S. $\frac{1}{4}$ cup) butter
150 g/5 oz (U.S. $\frac{2}{3}$ cup) sugar
175 g/6 oz plain flour (U.S. 1$\frac{1}{2}$ cups all-purpose flour)
2 teaspoons baking powder
$\frac{1}{4}$ teaspoon salt
grated rind and juice of 1 large lemon
5 tablespoons (U.S. 6 tablespoons) milk
1 egg, beaten
Topping
25 g/1 oz plain flour (U.S. $\frac{1}{4}$ cup all-purpose flour)
1 teaspoon ground ginger
2 teaspoons cocoa powder (U.S. 2 teaspoons
unsweetened cocoa)
50 g/2 oz (U.S. $\frac{1}{4}$ cup) butter
75 g/3 oz (U.S. 6 tablespoons) brown sugar

Cream the butter with the sugar until light and fluffy.
Sift the flour with the baking powder and salt, and fold
into the creamed mixture with the lemon rind and juice.
Finally add the milk and egg, mixing well. Spoon into a
greased 18-cm/7-inch round cake or soufflé dish and
level the surface.

Prepare the topping by sifting the flour with the
ginger and cocoa powder. Rub in the butter until the
mixture resembles fine breadcrumbs. Stir in the brown
sugar.

Cook the cake mixture for 3 minutes, giving the dish
a quarter turn every $\frac{3}{4}$ minute. Sprinkle over the cake
topping and cook for a further 3 minutes, giving the
dish a half turn every 1 minute. Allow to cool slightly,
then turn out onto a wire rack to cool.

Cut into wedges to serve. **Makes 1 (18-cm/7-inch)
round cake**

Tropical Christmas cake ring

Power setting Full and Low
Total cooking time 25$\frac{3}{4}$–31 minutes

Cake
175 g/6 oz (U.S. $\frac{3}{4}$ cup) butter, softened
100 g/4 oz (U.S. $\frac{2}{3}$ cup) brown sugar
2 large/size 1 or 2 eggs, beaten
225 g/8 oz self-raising flour (U.S. 2 cups all-purpose
flour sifted with 2 teaspoons baking powder)
75 g/3 oz glacé cherries (U.S. $\frac{1}{3}$ cup candied cherries)
quartered
75 g/3 oz (U.S. $\frac{1}{2}$ cup) chopped mixed candied peel
100 g/4 oz sultanas (U.S. $\frac{3}{4}$ cup seedless white raisins)
25 g/1 oz desiccated coconut (U.S. $\frac{1}{3}$ cup shredded
coconut)
25 g/1 oz (U.S. 2 tablespoons) angelica, chopped
25 g/1 oz (U.S. $\frac{1}{4}$ cup) shelled walnuts, chopped
1 (227-g/8-oz) can pineapple slices
Icing
40 g/1$\frac{1}{2}$ oz (U.S. 3 tablespoons) butter
175 g/6 oz icing sugar, sifted (U.S. 1$\frac{1}{3}$ cups sifted
confectioners' sugar)
25 g/1 oz desiccated coconut (U.S. $\frac{1}{3}$ cup shredded
coconut)
Decoration
glacé cherries (candied cherries)
glacé apricots (candied apricots)
angelica

Cream the butter with the sugar until light and fluffy.
Beat in the eggs with a little flour, mixing well. Add the
fruits alternately with the flour. Mix in the coconut,
angelica and walnuts. Drain the pineapple, reserving the
juice. Chop the flesh finely and add to the cake mixture
with 3 tablespoons (U.S. $\frac{1}{4}$ cup) of the pineapple juice.

Spoon into a greased 1.4-litre/2$\frac{1}{2}$-pint (U.S. 6$\frac{1}{4}$-cup)
glass ring mould, levelling the surface. Cook on *Low
Power* for 25–30 minutes, giving the dish a quarter turn
every 5 minutes, or until a wooden cocktail stick
inserted into the centre of the cake comes out clean.
Leave to stand for 30 minutes, then turn out onto a wire
rack to cool.

For the icing, place the butter in a bowl and cook on
Full Power for $\frac{3}{4}$–1 minute to melt. Add the icing sugar,
coconut and 1 tablespoon pineapple juice. Stir well then
spread quickly on top of the cake. Fork lightly to give a
frosty appearance and decorate with ribbon if liked,
glacé cherries, apricots and angelica. **Serves 8–10**

Variation
It is possible to make this cake in a deep 20-cm/8-inch
round cake or soufflé dish. Prepare as above but cook on
Low Power for 30–35 minutes. Decorate as above.

Sunshine savarin

Power setting Full and Medium
Total cooking time 16¼–18¼ minutes

1 teaspoon sugar
150 ml/¼ pint (U.S. ⅔ cup) water
2 teaspoons dried yeast (U.S. 2 teaspoons active dry yeast)
225 g/8 oz plain flour (U.S. 2 cups all-purpose flour)
½ teaspoon salt
50 g/2 oz (U.S. ¼ cup) butter
2 eggs, beaten
4 tablespoons (U.S. ⅓ cup) clear honey
4 tablespoons (U.S. ⅓ cup) brown rum
4 tablespoons (U.S. ⅓ cup) apricot jam
2 tablespoons (U.S. 3 tablespoons) water
whipped cream and prepared fresh fruits to serve

Place the sugar and water in a jug. Cook on *Full Power* for ½ minute. Add the yeast and leave until frothy.

Sift the flour with the salt. Add the yeast liquid and mix to a soft dough. Cover and leave to rise until doubled.

Place the butter in a bowl and cook on *Full Power* for 1½ minutes. Beat in the eggs and butter and pour into a greased 20-cm/8-inch glass ring mould. Cover and leave until well risen in the mould. Cook on *Medium Power* for 10–12 minutes, rotating every 3 minutes.

Meanwhile for the syrup, place the honey, rum, apricot jam and water in a bowl. Cover and cook on *Full Power* for 4 minutes. Brush over the savarin. Cool then decorate with the cream and fruits. **Serves 8**

Lemon shortbread fans

Power setting Full
Total cooking time 3–4 minutes

100 g/4 oz (U.S. ½ cup) butter
65 g/2½ oz (U.S. 5 tablespoons) brown granulated sugar
150 g/5 oz plain flour (U.S. 1¼ cups all-purpose flour)
3 tablespoons (U.S. ¼ cup) rice flour
½ teaspoon salt
½ teaspoon baking powder
Topping
grated rind of ½ lemon
1 tablespoon brown granulated sugar

Cream the butter with the sugar until light and fluffy. Sift the flour with the rice flour, salt and baking powder. Work into the creamed mixture to form a dough.

Line a 18-cm/7-inch fluted flan dish (U.S. 7-inch pie dish) with cling film. Press the dough into the dish and smooth the top. Mark into 8 wedges or fans. Sprinkle with the lemon rind and sugar, pressing it lightly into the shortbread.

Cook for 3–4 minutes, giving the dish a quarter turn every 1 minute. Allow to cool slightly, cut into wedges, then turn out onto a wire rack to cool. **Makes 8**

Golden chocolate and banana cake

Power setting Full
Total cooking time 9–10 minutes

100 g/4 oz (U.S. $\frac{1}{2}$ cup) margarine
275 g/10 oz (U.S. $1\frac{1}{4}$ cups) brown granulated sugar
2 eggs, beaten
275 g/10 oz self-raising flour (U.S. $2\frac{1}{2}$ cups all-purpose flour sifted with $2\frac{1}{2}$ teaspoons baking powder)
50 g/2 oz cocoa powder (U.S. $\frac{1}{2}$ cup unsweetened cocoa)
$\frac{3}{4}$ teaspoon bicarbonate of soda (U.S. $\frac{3}{4}$ teaspoon baking soda) blended with $\frac{1}{2}$ teaspoon salt
4 ripe bananas, peeled and mashed
3 tablespoons (U.S. $\frac{1}{4}$ cup) natural yogurt
150 ml/$\frac{1}{4}$ pint double cream (U.S. $\frac{2}{3}$ cup heavy cream)

Cream the margarine with the sugar. Beat in the eggs, mixing well. Sift the flour with the cocoa powder, bicarbonate of soda and salt, and fold into the creamed mixture. Mix half of the bananas with the yogurt and fold in. Line 2 (20-cm/8-inch) shallow cake dishes with cling film. Divide the mixture evenly between them. Cook, one at a time, for $4\frac{1}{2}$–5 minutes, giving the dish a half turn every 1 minute. Allow to stand for 5 minutes, then turn out on a wire rack to cool.

For the filling, whip the cream until stiff. Add the remaining banana. Sandwich the cakes together with the mixture. Decorate with sliced banana. **Serves 6**

Overnight chocolate cake

Power setting Full
Total cooking time 3–4 minutes

225 g/8 oz (U.S. 1 cup) unsalted butter, diced
225 g/8 oz plain dessert chocolate (U.S. $1\frac{1}{3}$ cups semi-sweet chocolate pieces)
2 eggs, beaten
25 g/1 oz castor sugar (U.S. 2 tablespoons sugar)
12 Nice biscuits
50 g/2 oz glacé cherries (U.S. $\frac{1}{4}$ cup candied cherries), chopped
50 g/2 oz (U.S. $\frac{1}{2}$ cup) shelled walnuts, chopped
Decoration
whipped cream
crystallised orange slices

Place the butter and chocolate in a bowl. Cook for 3–4 minutes until completely melted, stirring every 1 minute. Add the eggs and sugar and beat to blend well.

Line a 450-g/1-lb loaf tin with non-stick greaseproof paper. Layer the chocolate mixture, biscuits, cherries and nuts in the tin, starting and finishing with a layer of the chocolate mixture. Chill overnight until firm.

To serve, turn out onto a serving plate. Decorate with swirls of whipped cream and crystallised orange slices. **Serves 8**

Puddings and Desserts

If a main course is the anchor of a meal then the pudding or dessert is the crowning glory. The microwave will ensure you sweet-toothed success with its vast array of fruit, sponge or pastry puddings on offer. Even those time-consuming winter favourites like roly-poly puddings, crumbles and custards can be made in minutes rather than hours.

And not forgetting the refrigerator or freezer. The microwave will make light work of preparing ice creams, mousses, cheesecakes and caramels.

Remember to prick or score whole fruits prior to cooking in the microwave to allow any steam to escape or the fruits may explode with the pressure that builds up during cooking, and turn or rotate at regular intervals for good results.

In most cases it is recommended that you cover puddings and desserts during cooking – if this is an irregular-shaped dish, use grease-proof paper with an elastic band or cling film.

Guide to cooking fruit

Fruit	Quantity	Preparation	Cooking time in minutes on Full power
Cooking apples	450 g (1 lb)	Peel, core and slice. Sprinkle with 100 g/4 oz (U.S. ½ cup) sugar.	6–8
Baked apples or Pears	1 2 3 4	Core and score the apples or pears around their circumference with a sharp knife to prevent bursting.	2–4 4–5½ 6–8 9–10
Apricots	450 g (1 lb)	Stone and wash. Sprinkle with 100 g/4 oz (U.S. ½ cup) sugar.	6–8
Gooseberries	450 g (1 lb)	Top and tail. Sprinkle with 100 g/4 oz (U.S. ½ cup) sugar.	4–5
Peaches	4 medium-sized	Stone and wash. Sprinkle with 100 g/4 oz (U.S. ½ cup) sugar.	4–5
Pears	6 medium-sized	Peel, halve and core. Dissolve 75 g/3 oz (U.S. 6 tablespoons) sugar in a little water and pour over pears.	8–10

Fruit	Quantity	Time in minutes on Full power	Time in minutes on Defrost power
Plums, Cherries, Damsons or Greengages	450 g (1 lb)	Stone and wash. Sprinkle with 100 g/4 oz (U.S. ½ cup) sugar and the grated rind of ½ lemon.	4–6
Soft berry fruits	450 g (1 lb)	Top and tail or hull. Wash and add 100 g/4 oz (U.S. ½ cup) sugar.	3–5
Rhubarb	450 g (1 lb)	Trim and cut into short lengths. Add 100 g/4 oz (U.S. ½ cup) sugar and the grated rind of 1 lemon.	9–10
Dry sugar pack fruit	450 g (1 lb)	4–8	—
Sugar syrup pack fruit	450 g (1 lb)	8–12	—
Free-flow or open-freeze fruit	450 g (1 lb)	—	4–8

Sponge summer pudding

(Illustrated on pages 154–155)

Power setting Full
Total cooking time 2½–3 minutes

450 g/1 lb (u.s. 3 cups) raspberries, hulled
450 g/1 lb redcurrants, topped and tailed (u.s. 4 cups red currants, stemmed and headed)
225 g/8 oz blackcurrants, topped and tailed (u.s. 2 cups black currants, stemmed and headed)
100 g/4 oz (u.s. scant 1 cup) blackberries, hulled
225 g/8 oz (u.s. 1 cup) sugar
6 tablespoons (u.s. ½ cup) water
16 trifle sponges

Place the raspberries, redcurrants, blackcurrants and blackberries in a bowl with the sugar and water. Cover and cook for 2½–3 minutes until softened. Allow to cool.

Line the bottom and sides of a 1.5-litre/2½-pint pudding basin or mould (u.s. 3-pint pudding mold) with the trifle sponges, trimming to make a neat fit. Cut the remaining trifle sponges in half. Layer the fruits and trifle sponges in the basin, finishing with a layer of trifle sponges. Cover the pudding with a plate and put a heavy weight on top to press the fruit down firmly. Chill in the refrigerator for about 6–8 hours or long enough for the juices to penetrate and soak the sponges.

To serve, turn the pudding out onto a serving dish and serve alone or with cream. **Serves 6**

Strawberry and tangerine mousses

(Illustrated on pages 154–155)

Power setting Full
Total cooking time 1 minute

6 trifle sponges
675 g/1½ lb (u.s. 5 cups) strawberries, hulled
finely grated rind and juice of 2 tangerines or 2 small sweet oranges
25 g/1 oz icing sugar (u.s. ¼ cup confectioners' sugar), sifted
3 egg yolks
100 g/4 oz castor sugar (u.s. ½ cup sugar)
1 tablespoon powdered gelatine (u.s. 1 envelope gelatin)
3 tablespoons (u.s. ¼ cup) water
150 ml/¼ pint (u.s. ⅔ cup) whipping cream
2 egg whites
Decoration
whipped cream
julienne strips of tangerine or orange rind

Line the bases of 6 individual glasses with the trifle sponges. Finely slice a third of the strawberries and use to line the sides of the glasses. Purée the remaining strawberries and sieve to remove any pips. Mix with the tangerine rind and juice and the icing sugar.

Whisk the egg yolks and castor sugar until thick and creamy. Whisk in the strawberry and tangerine mixture. Soak the gelatine in the water in a small bowl to soften for 2 minutes. Cook for ½ minute until the gelatine has dissolved. Allow to cool slightly then fold into the mousse. Whip the cream until it stands in soft peaks and, using a metal spoon, fold into the mousse.

Whisk the egg whites until they stand in stiff peaks. Fold into the mousse. Spoon the mousse into the dishes, taking care not to disturb the strawberries. Chill until set, about 2–4 hours.

When set, decorate the mousses with swirls of whipped cream and julienne strips of tangerine rind. **Serves 6**

Crunchy blackcurrant cheesecake

(Illustrated on pages 154–155)

Power setting Full
Total cooking time 2½ minutes

Biscuit base
75 g/3 oz (u.s. 6 tablespoons) butter
175 g/6 oz digestive biscuits, crushed (u.s. 2¼ cups graham cracker crumbs)
Cheesecake
175 g/6 oz (u.s. ¾ cup) cream cheese
50 g/2 oz castor sugar (u.s. ¼ cup sugar)
2 eggs, separated
15 g/½ oz gelatine (u.s. 2 envelopes gelatin)
3 tablespoons (u.s. ¼ cup) blackcurrant cordial
175 g/6 oz blackcurrants, topped and tailed (u.s. 1½ cups black currants, stemmed and headed)
150 ml/¼ pint (u.s. ⅔ cup) blackcurrant yogurt
150 ml/¼ pint (u.s. ⅔ cup) whipping cream

Place the butter in a bowl and cook for 2 minutes. Add the biscuit crumbs, mixing well. Grease and line the base and sides of a 22-cm/8-inch spring form cake tin with greaseproof paper. Press the crumbs onto the base and chill.

Meanwhile, beat the cream cheese and sugar together until creamy. Add the egg yolks. Soak the gelatine in the cordial. Cook for ½ minute. Allow to cool slightly then mix into the cheese mixture with the blackcurrants and yogurt. Whip the cream and fold into the blackcurrant mixture. Whisk the egg whites until stiff and fold in. Pour onto the biscuit crust and chill until set. Serve decorated with whipped cream and hazelnuts. **Serves 6–8**

Quick redcurrant gâteau

Power setting Full
Total cooking time 3½–4 minutes

1 ready-cooked sponge sandwich cake
2 egg yolks
20 g/¾ oz (U.S. 1½ tablespoons) sugar
20 g/¾ oz (U.S. 3 tablespoons) flour
15 g/½ oz cornflour (U.S. 1½ tablespoons cornstarch)
300 ml/½ pint (U.S. 1¼ cups) milk
4 tablespoons (U.S. ⅓ cup) redcurrant jelly
1 egg white
40 g/1½ oz castor sugar (U.S. 2 tablespoons sugar)
175 g/6 oz red currants, topped and tailed (U.S. 1½ cups red currants, stemmed and headed)

Using a sharp knife, carefully halve the sponge sandwich horizontally. Cut the top layer of the cake into six wedges and reserve. Mix the egg yolks with the sugar, flour, cornflour and a little of the milk. Place the remaining milk in a jug and cook for 2 minutes. Pour onto the egg paste, beating well. Cook for a further 1½–2 minutes until thickened. Stir in the redcurrant jelly, blending well and allow to cool.

When cool, whisk the egg white with the castor sugar until it stands in stiff peaks. Fold into the custard mixture with two-thirds of the redcurrants. Spoon the redcurrant cream onto the base of the sponge and top with the sponge wedges, positioned at an angle. Fill the centre of the top of the cake with the remaining redcurrants. Chill before serving, about 30 minutes.

Cut between the sponge wedges to serve. **Serves 6**

Variations
Quick raspberry gâteau Prepare and cook as above but use 4 tablespoons seedless raspberry jam (U.S. ⅓ cup seedless raspberry jelly) instead of the redcurrant jelly and 175 g/6 oz (U.S. 1 cup) raspberries instead of the redcurrants.
Quick strawberry gâteau Prepare and cook as above but use 4 tablespoons strawberry jam (U.S. ⅓ cup strawberry jelly) instead of the redcurrant jelly and 175 g/6 oz (U.S. 1 cup) sliced or whole strawberries instead of the redcurrants.
Quick blackcurrant gâteau Prepare and cook as above but use 4 tablespoons seedless blackcurrant jam (U.S. ⅓ cup seedless blackcurrant jelly) instead of the redcurrant jelly and 175 g/6 oz (U.S. 1½ cups) blackcurrants instead of the redcurrants.
Quick peach gâteau Prepare and cook as above but use 4 tablespoons apricot or peach jam (U.S. ⅓ cup apricot or peach jelly) instead of the redcurrant jelly and 2 peeled, stoned and finely sliced peaches instead of the redcurrants.

Upside-down raspberry trifle

Power setting Full
Total cooking time 2–2½ minutes

3 tablespoons custard powder (U.S. ¼ cup Bird's English dessert mix)
3 tablespoons (U.S. ¼ cup) sugar
150 ml/¼ pint (U.S. ⅔ cup) milk
25 g/1 oz (U.S. 2 tablespoons) butter
1 teaspoon almond essence
2 eggs, separated
12 trifle sponges
150 ml/¼ pint double cream (U.S. ⅔ cup heavy cream)
150 g/5 oz (U.S. 1 cup) raspberries, hulled
whipped cream and chopped nuts to decorate

Mix the custard powder with the sugar and a little milk to make a smooth paste. Cook the remaining milk in a jug for 1 minute. Pour onto the paste, stirring well. Cook for a further 1–1½ minutes, stirring every ½ minute until very thick and smooth. Beat in the butter, almond essence and egg yolks. Allow to cool.

Slice the trifle sponges in half horizontally. Press 12 halves, cut sides out, around the base and sides of a 1.5-litre/2½-pint pudding basin (U.S. 6¼-cup pudding mold) to completely line it.

Whip the cream until it stands in soft peaks and fold into the cool custard. Stir in two-thirds of the raspberries. Whisk the egg whites until they stand in soft peaks and fold into the raspberry mixture. Pour one-third of the mixture into the basin. Cover with 3½ cut trifle sponge halves. Repeat once then finally cover with the remaining 5 cut trifle sponge halves. Cover the top of the pudding with a plate and weight to firmly push down the cream. Chill overnight or for 8 hours.

To serve, turn the pudding out onto a serving plate. Decorate with whipped cream, chopped nuts and the remaining raspberries. **Serves 6–8**

Variations
Upside-down strawberry trifle Prepare and cook as above but use 150 g/5 oz (U.S. 1 cup) sliced strawberries instead of the raspberries.
Upside-down gooseberry trifle Prepare and cook as above but use 150 g/5 oz (U.S. 1 cup) cooked and sweetened gooseberries instead of the raspberries.
Upside-down cherry trifle Prepare and cook as above but use 150 g/5 oz stoned fresh or canned cherries (U.S. 1 cup pitted fresh or canned cherries) instead of the raspberries.

Chocolate pudding

Power setting Full
Total cooking time 11½–13½ minutes

190 g/6½ oz (U.S. ¾ cup plus 1 tablespoon) butter
175 g/6 oz (U.S. ¾ cup) sugar
3 large/size 1 or 2 eggs, beaten
190 g/6½ oz self-raising flour (U.S. 1½ cups plus 2
tablespoons all-purpose flour sifted with 1½ teaspoons
baking powder)
25 g/1 oz cocoa powder (U.S. ¼ cup unsweetened
cocoa), sifted
50 g/2 oz plain chocolate (U.S. ⅓ cup semi-sweet
chocolate pieces), grated
Sauce
grated rind and juice of 2 large oranges
1 tablespoon sugar
150 ml/¼ pint (U.S. ⅔ cup) water
15 g/½ oz (U.S. 1 tablespoon) butter
15 g/½ oz plain flour (U.S. 2 tablespoons all-purpose)

Cream the butter with the sugar until fluffy. Beat in the
eggs with the flour. Add the cocoa powder and grated
chocolate. Spoon into a greased 1.4-litre/2½-pint pudding basin (U.S. 6¼-cup pudding mold). Cook for 6–7
minutes until well risen and cooked through.

Mix the orange rind and juice, sugar and water in a
jug. Cook for 3 minutes. Place the butter in a bowl and
cook for ½ minute. Stir in the flour. Gradually add the
orange mixture. Cook for 2–3 minutes, stirring every ½
minute. Serve topped with the sauce. **Serves 4–6**

Golden pudding

Power setting Full
Total cooking time 6–7 minutes

100 g/4 oz (U.S. ½ cup) butter
100 g/4 oz (U.S. ½ cup) sugar
2 eggs, beaten
100 g/4 oz self-raising flour (U.S. 1 cup all-purpose
flour sifted with 1 teaspoon baking powder)
grated rind and juice ½ lemon
75 g/3 oz golden syrup (U.S. ¼ cup light corn syrup)
2 lemons, peeled, pith removed and sliced
extra golden syrup or custard to serve

Cream the butter with the sugar until light and fluffy.
Beat in the eggs, mixing well. Fold the flour into the
mixture with the lemon rind and juice.

Spoon 1 tablespoon of the golden syrup into a well-
greased, 900-ml/1½-pint pudding basin (U.S. 4-cup
pudding mold). Arrange half the lemon slices neatly in
the base of the bowl. Cover with half of the sponge
mixture. Cover with the remaining lemon slices and
golden syrup, then top with the remaining sponge
mixture. Cover with cling film, snipping two holes in
the top for the steam to escape. Cook for 6–7 minutes,
giving the bowl a half turn after 3 minutes. Leave to
stand for 5–10 minutes, then turn out onto a heated
serving plate.

Cut into wedges and serve with extra golden syrup or
pouring custard. **Serves 4–6**

Christmas pudding

Power setting Full
Total cooking time 8 minutes

75 g/3 oz (U.S. 1½ cups) fresh white breadcrumbs
75 g/3 oz plain flour (U.S. ¾ cup all-purpose flour)
½ teaspoon ground mixed spice
75 g/3 oz (U.S. ⅔ cup) shredded suet
100 g/4 oz soft brown sugar (U.S. ⅔ cup light brown)
50 g/2 oz (U.S. ⅓ cup) chopped mixed candied peel
75 g/3 oz (U.S. ½ cup) currants
50 g/2 oz sultanas (U.S. ⅓ cup seedless white raisins)
150 g/5 oz (U.S. 1 cup) raisins
40 g/1½ oz (U.S. ⅓ cup) blanched almonds, chopped
1 small cooking apple, peeled, cored and chopped
grated rind and juice of ½ lemon
1 tablespoon brandy
1 large/size 1 or 2 egg, beaten
2½ tablespoons brown ale (U.S. 3 tablespoons dark beer)
1 tablesppon milk
1½ tablespoons black treacle (U.S. 2 tablespoons molasses)

Mix the breadcrumbs with the flour, mixed spice, suet, sugar, peel, currants, sultanas, raisins, almonds and apple. Add the lemon rind and juice, brandy, egg, ale, milk and treacle, mixing well. Cover and leave overnight.

Turn into a greased 1.15-litre/2-pint pudding basin (U.S. 2½-pint pudding mold). Cover loosely with cling film and cook for 8 minutes. Leave to stand for 5 minutes before turning out to serve. **Serves 4–6**

Crunchy fruit crumble

Power setting Full
Total cooking time 11–13 minutes

450 g/1 lb rhubarb, sliced (or peeled, cored and sliced apples, halved and stoned plums, or topped and tailed gooseberries)
150 g/5 oz (U.S. ⅔ cup) brown sugar
75 g/3 oz (U.S. 6 tablespoons) butter
100 g/4 oz (U.S. 1 cup) wholewheat flour
50 g/2 oz (U.S. ⅔ cup) rolled oats
½ teaspoon ground cinnamon

Place the rhubarb in a dish and sprinkle with 50 g/2 oz (U.S. ¼ cup) of the sugar.

Rub the butter into the flour until the mixture resembles fine breadcrumbs. Stir in the remaining sugar, oats and cinnamon, mixing well. Carefully spoon on top of the fruit and cook for 11–13 minutes, giving the dish a quarter turn every 3 minutes. Brown under a preheated hot grill if liked.

Serve with cream, custard or ice cream as liked.
Serves 4

Blackberry fool

Power setting Full
Total cooking time 4–5 minutes

450 g/1 lb (U.S. 3 cups) blackberries, hulled
75 g/3 oz (U.S. ⅓ cup) brown sugar
juice of 1 small lemon
1 tablespoon water
300 ml/½ pint double cream (U.S. 1¼ cups heavy cream)

Wash the blackberries and place in a dish, reserving a few for decoration. Add the sugar, lemon juice and water. Cover and cook for 4–5 minutes until soft. Allow to cool then purée in a blender. Sieve to remove any pips. Chill thoroughly.

Whip the cream until it stands in firm peaks. Reserve a little of the cream for decoration and fold the remainder into the blackberry purée with a metal spoon. Spoon into four individual serving dishes. Top with a swirl of the reserved cream and the reserved blackberries. **Serves 4**

Variations

Blackcurrant fool Prepare and cook as above but use topped and tailed blackcurrants instead of the blackberries.

Raspberry fool Prepare and cook as above but use hulled raspberries instead of the blackberries.

Strawberry fool Prepare and cook as above but use hulled strawberries instead of the blackberries.

Blackberry and apple fool Prepare and cook as above but use 225 g/8 oz (U.S. 2 cups) peeled, cored and diced cooking apple instead of 225 g/8 oz (U.S. 1½ cups) of the blackberries. Cover and cook for 6–8 minutes until soft.

Gooseberry fool Prepare as above but use topped and tailed gooseberries instead of the blackberries. Prick the gooseberries before cooking. Cover and cook for 6 minutes until soft.

Crunchy pear layer

Power setting Full
Total cooking time 14½–17 minutes

450 g/1 lb pears, peeled, cored and quartered
3 tablespoons (U.S. ¼ cup) water
2 teaspoons ground ginger
150 g/5 oz (U.S. ¾ cup) brown sugar
50 g/2 oz (U.S. ¼ cup) butter
150 g/5 oz (U.S. 2½ cups) fresh white or brown breadcrumbs
pear slices to decorate

Place the pears in a dish with the water, ginger and 50 g/2 oz (U.S. ⅓ cup) of the sugar. Cover and cook for 8–10 minutes until tender.

Preheat a large browning dish or skillet for 5 minutes (or according to manufacturer's instructions). Quickly add the butter to the dish and swirl to coat the dish and melt. Add the breadcrumbs and remaining sugar and cook for 4 minutes, stirring halfway through the cooking time.

Layer the pears and crunchy crumbs in four individual dishes. Cook for 2½–3 minutes until hot. Place under a preheated hot grill to brown the tops if liked. Decorate with pear slices. **Serves 4**

Variations

Crunchy apple and cinnamon layer Prepare as above but use 450 g/1 lb peeled, cored and thickly-sliced cooking apples instead of the pears and 2 teaspoons ground cinnamon instead of the ginger. Omit the water. Cover and cook for 6–8 minutes until tender.

Crunchy apple and blackberry layer Prepare and cook as above but use 225 g/8 oz (U.S. 2 cups) peeled, cored and thickly-sliced cooking apples with 225 g/8 oz (U.S. 1½ cups) hulled blackberries. Omit the water and replace the ginger with the grated rind of ½ lemon. Cover and cook for 6–8 minutes until tender.

Crunchy rhubarb layer Prepare as above but use 450 g/1 lb sliced rhubarb instead of the pears and the finely grated rind of ½ small orange instead of the ginger. Omit the water. Cover and cook for 10 minutes until tender.

Pears Helène

Power setting Full
Total cooking time 9½–12 minutes

4 trifle sponges
2 tablespoons (U.S. 3 tablespoons) chocolate and
hazelnut spread
2 large dessert pears, peeled, cored and halved
50 g/2 oz (U.S. 2 tablespoons) clear honey
4 tablespoons (U.S. ⅓ cup) water
100 g/4 oz plain dessert or ordinary chocolate (U.S. ⅔
cup semi-sweet chocolate pieces)
Decoration
150 ml/¼ pint double cream (U.S. ⅔ cup heavy
cream), whipped
chopped nuts
chocolate leaves

Using a sharp knife, halve the trifle sponges horizont-ally. Sandwich together again with the chocolate and hazelnut spread. Stand each sponge in an individual serving dish.

Place the pears in a dish with the honey and water. Cover and cook for 8–10 minutes until tender. Cool and drain well, reserving the syrup.

Place the chocolate in a bowl and cook for 1½–2 minutes until just melted. Spoon a little syrup over the trifle sponges and place a pear half on top of each. Dribble the chocolate over the pears in a zig-zag pattern. Chill until set.

Serve decorated with a swirl of whipped cream, chopped nuts and chocolate leaves. **Serves 4**

Plum and rhubarb crispbread crumble

Power setting Full
Total cooking time 13 minutes

4 large ripe plums, halved and stoned
225 g/8 oz (U.S. ½ lb) rhubarb, cut into bite-sized
pieces
2 tablespoons (U.S. 3 tablespoons) water
100 g/4 oz (U.S. ½ cup) sugar
grated rind of 1 lemon
7 rye light crispbreads, coarsely crushed
¼ teaspoon ground cinnamon
grated rind of 1 orange
25 g/1 oz (U.S. 2 tablespoons) butter
25 g/1 oz (U.S. ¼ cup) shelled walnuts, coarsely
chopped
50 g/2 oz (U.S. ¼ cup) sugar
orange slices to decorate

Place the plums and rhubarb in a dish with the water, sugar and lemon rind. Cover and cook for 8 minutes, stirring halfway through the cooking time.

Mix the crushed crispbreads with the cinnamon and orange rind. Place the butter in a small dish and cook for 1 minute to melt. Stir the melted butter into the crispbread mixture. Fold in the nuts and sugar. Spoon the crumble mixture evenly over the fruit. Cook for 4 minutes until hot. Decorate with orange slices. **Serves 4**

Variations
Bramble crispbread crumble Prepare as above but mix equal quantities of redcurrants, blackcurrants and other berry fruits to make up to 450 g/1 lb (U.S. 3 cups). Omit the water. Cover and cook for 4–5 minutes until just tender.
Gooseberry and orange crispbread crumble Prepare as above but use 450 g/1 lb gooseberries and the finely grated rind of 1 orange instead of the plums and rhubarb. Prick the gooseberries before cooking. Cover and cook for 6 minutes.
Spicy peach crispbread crumble Prepare as above but use 4 large skinned, stoned and thickly sliced peaches instead of the plums and rhubarb. Cover and cook for 4–6 minutes. Use ¼ teaspoon ground mixed spice instead of the ground cinnamon in the crispbread topping.

Blackberry wine rosy syllabub

Power setting Full
Total cooking time 3 minutes

350 g/12 oz (U.S. 2¼ cups) blackberries, hulled
150 ml/¼ pint (U.S. ⅔ cup) rosé wine
2 tablespoons (U.S. 3 tablespoons) lemon juice
2 teaspoons finely grated lemon rind
75 g/3 oz castor sugar (U.S. 6 tablespoons sugar)
300 ml/½ pint double cream (U.S. 1¼ cups heavy cream)
sponge fingers (U.S. ladyfingers) to serve (optional)

Place the blackberries in a bowl with the wine, lemon juice and rind and sugar. Cover and cook for 3 minutes. Allow to cool.

Remove the blackberries with a slotted spoon and place in the bases of four sundae glasses. Add the cream to the cool wine mixture and whip until the mixture stands in soft peaks. Swirl on top of the blackberries and chill lightly. Serve with sponge fingers if liked. **Serves 4**

Creamy ice cream

Power setting Full
Total cooking time 6 minutes

450 ml/¾ pint (U.S. 2 cups) milk
2 eggs, beaten
175 g/6 oz (U.S. ¾ cup) sugar
1 tablespoon vanilla essence (U.S. 1 tablespoon vanilla extract)
300 ml/½ pint double cream (U.S. 1¼ cups heavy cream)
sweet crisp biscuits to serve

Beat the milk with the eggs and sugar in a bowl. Cook for 6 minutes, stirring every 2 minutes to make a smooth custard-like sauce. Allow to cool. Stir in the vanilla essence, mixing well. Lightly whip the cream until it stands in soft peaks. Fold into the custard mixture and pour into a freezer tray. Freeze until slushy, then whisk until smooth. Return to the freezer tray and freeze until firm.

Remove from the freezer and place in the refrigerator for about ½–1 hour before required. Serve scooped with sweet crisp biscuits. **Serves 4**

Variation
Fresh raspberry ice cream Prepare and cook as above but add 100 g/4 oz (U.S. 1 cup) raspberries, puréed and sieved, before the second freezing, swirling it through the smooth ice cream leaving a rosy streaked effect.

Chocolate and cherry cookie castles

Power setting Full
Total cooking time 2 minutes

100 g/4 oz milk or plain chocolate flavour cake covering (U.S. 4 squares semi-sweet chocolate)
100 g/4 oz (U.S. $\frac{1}{2}$ cup) butter
1 egg, beaten
25 g/1 oz demerara sugar (U.S. scant $\frac{1}{4}$ cup brown sugar)
225 g/8 oz (U.S. $\frac{1}{2}$ lb) chocolate chip and hazelnut cookies, coarsely broken
50 g/2 oz glacé cherries (U.S. $\frac{1}{4}$ cup candied cherries)
grated rind of 1 orange
Decoration
whipped cream
whole hazelnuts

Place the chocolate and butter in a bowl. Cook for 2 minutes to melt, stirring halfway through the cooking time. Beat the egg and sugar until well blended, then gradually add the melted chocolate mixture. Stir in the broken biscuits, cherries and orange rind. Press the mixture into 6 lightly oiled dariole moulds and leave to set in the refrigerator for about 3 hours.

To serve, dip the moulds quickly in hot water and invert onto serving dishes. Top with a swirl of cream and a hazelnut. Decorate the base of each castle with cream if liked. **Serves 6**

Lemon sorbet shells

Power setting Full
Total cooking time 5–6 minutes

2 teaspoons powdered gelatine (U.S. $\frac{2}{3}$ envelope gelatin)
300 ml/$\frac{1}{2}$ pint (U.S. 1$\frac{1}{4}$ cups) water
175 g/6 oz (U.S. $\frac{3}{4}$ cup) sugar
6 lemons
2 egg whites
mint sprigs to decorate
crispbread or wafer triangles to serve

Soak the gelatine in 3 tablespoons (U.S. $\frac{1}{4}$ cup) of the water. Place the remaining water in a deep bowl with the sugar. Cook for 5–6 minutes to make a syrup. Stir in the gelatine and leave to cool.

Cut a 'lid' about a third of the way down each lemon. Scoop out the flesh, using a teaspoon, into a bowl. Strain off the juice to make up to 300 ml/$\frac{1}{2}$ pint (U.S. 1$\frac{1}{4}$ cups) with water if necessary. Add the lemon juice to the syrup mixture and grate about 2 teaspoons of rind from the lemon lids and add to the syrup, mixing well. Whisk the egg whites until they stand in stiff peaks and fold into the syrup mixture. Pour into a freezer tray and freeze for 1$\frac{1}{4}$ hours. Beat until slushy then freeze for a further 1$\frac{1}{2}$ hours.

Wash the lemon skins and dry well. Spoon the sorbet into the lemon shells. Decorate with sprigs of mint and serve with crispbread or wafer triangles. **Serves 6**

Peach and orange chiffon

Power setting Full
Total cooking time 7–8 minutes

1 (135-g/4¾-oz) packet orange jelly tablet (U.S. 1 × 4 oz package orange-flavored gelatin)
300 ml/½ pint (U.S. 1¼ cups) water
5 fresh peaches, skinned, halved and stoned
50 g/2 oz (U.S. ¼ cup) sugar
300 ml/½ pint double cream (U.S. 1¼ cups heavy cream)
Decoration
16 sponge fingers (U.S. 16 ladyfingers)
fresh peach slices

Place the jelly in a jug with half of the water. Cook for 2–3 minutes until the jelly has dissolved.

Place the peaches in a dish with the remaining water and the sugar. Cover and cook for 5 minutes. Remove the peaches with a slotted spoon. Make the jelly up to 450 ml/¾ pint (U.S. 2 cups) with the peach syrup. Allow to cool until almost set.

Chop the peaches coarsely. Whip the cream until it stands in soft peaks. Whisk the setting jelly until foamy, then whisk in the cream. Fold the chopped peach into the jelly mixture and turn into a 675-g/1½-lb loaf tin. Chill until set.

To serve, immerse the loaf tin briefly in hot water, turn out onto a serving dish. Decorate the sides of the chiffon with the sponge fingers and the top with slices of fresh peach. **Serves 4–6**

Raspberry and apricot flan

Power setting Full
Total cooking time 15–15½ minutes

100 g/4 oz (U.S. ½ cup) sugar
150 ml/¼ pint (U.S. ⅔ cup) water
350 g/12 oz (U.S. ¾ lb) apricots, halved and stoned
2 egg yolks
50 g/2 oz castor sugar (U.S. ¼ cup sugar)
grated rind of 1 orange
1½ tablespoons cornflour (U.S. 2 tablespoons cornstarch)
1½ tablespoons plain flour (U.S. 2 tablespoons all-purpose flour)
300 ml/½ pint (U.S. 1¼ cups) milk
1 egg white
350 g/12 oz (U.S. 2½ cups) raspberries, hulled
1 large sponge flan case

Mix the sugar with the water in a bowl. Cook for 2 minutes to dissolve the sugar. Add the apricots. Cover and cook for 6 minutes. Remove the apricots with a slotted spoon and leave to cool. Cook the syrup, uncovered, for a further 3 minutes until syrupy. Leave to cool.

Meanwhile whisk the egg yolks with half the castor sugar until thick. Beat in the orange rind, cornflour and flour. Place the milk in a jug and cook for 2 minutes. Slowly pour the milk over the egg mixture, beating constantly. Cook for a further 2–2½ minutes, stirring every 1 minute until thickened and smooth. Leave to cool.

Whisk the egg white until it stands in soft peaks. Whisk in the remaining castor sugar until thick and glossy. Fold into the cooled orange mixture using a metal spoon. Crush half of the raspberries with a fork until soft and fold through the mixture. Spoon into the flan case, rounding it slightly in the centre.

Top with the apricot halves and the remaining raspberries. Brush with the cooled thickened syrup. **Serves 8**

Frozen yogurt trifle

Power setting Full
Total cooking time 2 minutes

16 sponge finger biscuits (U.S. 16 ladyfingers)
3 tablespoons (U.S. ¼ cup) brandy or orange juice
4 miniature jam Swiss rolls (U.S. 4 miniature jam jelly rolls)
300 ml/½ pint (U.S. 1¼ cups) natural yogurt
225 g/8 oz (U.S. 1½ cups) strawberries
50 g/2 oz icing sugar (U.S. ½ cup confectioners' sugar)
8 macaroon biscuits, crushed
4 tablespoons (U.S. ⅓ cup) strawberry jam

Line the base of an 18-cm/7-inch charlotte mould with a piece of foil. Dip the unsugared sides of the sponge fingers in the brandy or orange juice and use to line the sides of the mould, unsugared sides facing in. Slice the miniature jam rolls and line the base with about half of them. Top with half of the natural yogurt.

Place the strawberries and icing sugar in a bowl. Cover and cook for 2 minutes. Mash to a purée and allow to cool. Fold the cooled strawberries into the remaining yogurt.

Freeze the charlotte trifle until just firm. Sprinkle the frozen yogurt with the macaroons and spread over the jam. Pour over the strawberry yogurt, taking care not to disturb the macaroons and jam. Freeze until just firm, top with remaining sliced jam rolls. Freeze until firm.

To serve, carefully unmould the trifle onto a serving plate, removing the foil. Decorate with whipped cream and hazelnuts. Place in the refrigerator for about 1 hour before serving. Cut into wedges. **Serves 4–6**

Danish cream gâteau

Power setting Full
Total cooking time 2–3 minutes

100 g/4 oz (U.S. ½ cup) unsalted butter
150 ml/¼ pint (U.S. ⅔ cup) milk
½ teaspoon powdered gelatine
2 teaspoons water
2 teaspoons sugar
1 ready-cooked sponge cake
450 g/1 lb (U.S. 3 cups) strawberries, hulled
sugar to dust (optional)

Cut the butter into small pieces and place in a large jug with the milk. Cook for 2–3 minutes until melted, stirring every ½ minute, but do not let the mixture boil. Meanwhile, mix the gelatine with the water and leave to soften. Add a little of the melted butter and milk mixture to the softened gelatine and stir to mix. Return the gelatine mixture to the jug of milk and butter mixture and stir well to blend. Add the sugar and mix well. Pour this mixture into a liquidiser and blend on full speed for ½ minute. Pour into a bowl and chill for about 4 hours.

When well chilled, whisk the Danish cream until softly stiff and spread over the sponge cake. Decorate with the strawberries and dust with sugar if liked. Cut into thick wedges to serve. **Serves 6**

Variations
Butterscotch Danish cream gâteau Prepare and cook as above but fold 100 g/4 oz (U.S. ¼ lb) crushed praline or butterscotch into the whipped cream.
Cinnamon Danish cream gâteau Prepare and cook as above but add 1–2 teaspoons ground cinnamon to the cream before whipping.
Orange Danish cream gâteau Prepare and cook as above but add 1 tablespoon orange liqueur to the cream before whipping. Top the cream and gâteau with 4 peeled and segmented oranges instead of the strawberries.

St Clement's cheesecake

Power setting Full
Total cooking time 1½ minutes

Base
50 g/2 oz (U.S. ¼ cup) butter
8 large digestive biscuits (U.S. 8 large graham
crackers)
Topping
3 eggs, separated
75 g/3 oz (U.S. 6 tablespoons) sugar
6 tablespoons (U.S. ½ cup) lemon juice
15 g/½ oz powdered gelatine (U.S. 2 envelopes gelatin)
2 tablespoons (U.S. 3 tablespoons) water
225 g/8 oz (U.S. 1 cup) cream cheese
225 g/8 oz (U.S. 1 cup) cottage cheese, sieved
150 ml/¼ pint soured cream (U.S. ⅔ cup dairy sour
cream)
2 oranges, peeled and segmented

Place the butter in a bowl and cook for 1 minute to melt.
Add the biscuit crumbs and mix well. Spoon onto the
base of a 20-cm/8-inch spring form pan and chill to set.
Meanwhile, beat the egg yolks with the sugar and
lemon juice until very thick and creamy. Place the

gelatine in a small bowl with the water. Cook for ½
minute until clear and dissolved. Allow to cool slightly
then mix into the lemon mixture. Stir in the cream and
cottage cheeses with the soured cream, mixing well.

Whisk the egg whites until they stand in stiff peaks
then fold into the cheese mixture. Pour onto the biscuit
crust and chill until set.

To serve, unmould the cheesecake onto a serving
plate and decorate the top with orange segments. Cut
into wedges to serve. **Serves 6**

Variations
Three-fruit cheesecake Prepare and cook as above
but use 3 tablespoons (U.S. ¼ cup) grapefruit juice instead
of 3 tablespoons (U.S. ¼ cup) of the lemon juice. Decorate
the cheesecake with slices of grapefruit and orange
segments.
Lime and orange cheesecake Prepare and cook as
above but use 6 tablespoons (U.S. ½ cup) lime juice
instead of the lemon juice. Decorate with orange
segments and thin slices of lime.

Blackcurrant loaf

Power setting Full
Total cooking time 3½–4 minutes

350 g/12 oz blackcurrants, topped and tailed (U.S. 3
cups black currants, stemmed and headed)
100 g/4 oz (U.S. ½ cup) sugar
2 tablespoons (U.S. 3 tablespoons) water
2 eggs, separated
rind and juice of 1 lemon
25 g/1 oz powdered gelatine (U.S. 4 envelopes
gelatin)
150 ml/¼ pint double cream (U.S. ⅔ cup heavy cream)
28 sponge fingers (U.S. 28 ladyfingers)
whipped cream to decorate

Place two-thirds of the blackcurrants in a bowl with a
quarter of the sugar and the water. Cover and cook for 3
minutes. Cool then purée in a blender. Sieve to remove
any pips.

Whisk the egg yolks with the remaining sugar until
thick. Add the blackcurrant purée and lemon rind. Soak
the gelatine in the lemon juice in a bowl to soften for 2
minutes. Cook for ½–1 minute until the gelatine has
dissolved. Cool slightly then fold into the blackcurrant
mixture. Whip the cream until it stands in soft peaks.
Fold two-thirds of the cream into the blackcurrant
mixture. Whisk the egg whites until they stand in stiff
peaks. Fold into the blackcurrant mixture.

Place a layer of sponge fingers in the base of a 900-
g/2-lb loaf tin. Cover with a layer of blackcurrant
mixture. Top with another layer of fingers and blackcurrant mixture. Chill until set.

To serve, dip the mould briefly in hot water and
invert onto a serving plate. Spread the remaining
sponge fingers with the remaining cream and attach to
the sides of the blackcurrant loaf. Decorate with
coloured ribbon if liked, whipped cream and the
remaining whole blackcurrants. **Serves 8**

Strawberry and pistachio refrigerator cake

Power setting Full
Total cooking time 3 minutes

450 g/1 lb (U.S. 3 cups) strawberries, hulled
50 g/2 oz (U.S. ¼ cup) sugar
2 tablespoons (U.S. 3 tablespoons) water
28 sponge fingers (U.S. 28 ladyfingers)
300 ml/½ pint double cream (U.S. 1¼ cups heavy
cream)
2 tablespoons (U.S. 3 tablespoons) pistachio nuts

Slice the strawberries and place half in a dish with the
sugar and water. Cover and cook for 3 minutes. Cool
then purée in a blender until smooth. Sieve to remove
any pips.

Dip the sponge fingers, one at a time, into the
strawberry syrup. Arrange seven fingers, side by side,
on a serving plate. Whip half the cream until it stands in
soft peaks. Use a little to spread over the seven fingers.
Cover with a few pistachio nuts and sliced strawberries.
Repeat with the remaining fingers, using seven for each
layer, the cream, pistachio nuts and strawberries. Chill,
covered, for 2–4 hours.

To serve, whip the remaining cream and spread a
little over the top of the layered sponge fingers. Place
the remainder in a piping bag fitted with a star nozzle
and pipe cream shells across the top of the dessert. Slice
to serve. **Serves 6**

Jellies, Jams, Relishes and Sweets

Anyone who makes their own preserves and sweets will tell you just how rewarding it can be. But at what cost — steamy kitchens, bubbling and sticky pans and the great fear of scorching or burning. The microwave can take away those troublesome aspects leaving you with a quick, safe and convenient way to make preserves and sweets.

The procedures for making preserves and sweets in the microwave are very much the same as conventionally. You will need a large heatproof bowl, since mixtures do bubble up high, and sterilised jars.

The microwave will also help with a quick way to sterilise jars. Pour a little water into the base of each jar and cook each on *Full Power* for 2−3 minutes, depending upon size and thickness. Drain and leave upside down on absorbent kitchen towel until required.

To test for the setting point in jams and jellies, place a little of the mixture on a cold saucer. Allow to cool then push the mixture with the finger. If the surface wrinkles, setting point has been reached. If the surface does not wrinkle then cook longer. Several minutes of a good rolling boil are often required to achieve setting point. Commercial pectin can be used however in those fruit mixtures with a low pectin content. Follow the manu-facturer's instructions for use.

Apple jelly

Power setting Full
Total cooking time 17–21 minutes

475 ml/16 fl oz (U.S. 2 cups) unsweetened apple juice
800 g/1¾ lb (U.S. 3½ cups) sugar
5 tablespoons (U.S. 6 tablespoons) commercial pectin
green food colouring

Mix the apple juice with the sugar in a large heatproof bowl. Cover and cook for 12–14 minutes, stirring halfway through the cooking time.

Add the pectin, stirring well. Cover and cook for 4–6 minutes until the jelly mixture boils. Time for 1 minute boiling. Allow to cool slightly, removing any scum or foam. Tint with green food colouring and ladle into warm prepared jars. Cover, seal and label. **Makes about 2 (450-g/1 lb) jars**

Variations
Grape jelly Prepare and cook as above but use unsweetened grape juice instead of the apple juice. **Total cooking time 17–21 minutes**
Gooseberry jelly Place 1.8 kg/4 lb) gooseberries in a large bowl. Cover and cook until very soft, about 30 minutes. Strain the pulp through muslin. Measure the juice and place in a bowl with 450 g/1 lb (U.S. 2 cups) sugar to every 600 ml/1 pint (U.S. 2½ cups) juice. Add the pectin as above. Cover and cook for 4–6 minutes until the jelly mixture boils. Time for 1 minute boiling. Allow to cool slightly then ladle into warm prepared jars. Cover, seal and label. **Total cooking time 35–37 minutes**

Lemon curd

(Illustrated on pages 174–175)

Power setting Full and Low
Total cooking time 17–19 minutes

100 g/4 oz (U.S. ½ cup) butter
grated rind and juice of 3 lemons
225 g/8 oz (U.S. 1 cup) sugar
3 eggs
1 egg yolk

Mix the butter with the lemon rind and juice in a large heatproof bowl. Cook on *Full Power* for 3 minutes. Add the sugar, mixing well. Cook on *Full Power* for 2 minutes. Stir well to dissolve the sugar.

Beat the eggs and egg yolk together. Mix into the lemon mixture and cook, uncovered, on *Low Power* for 12–14 minutes, stirring every 3 minutes, until the mixture coats the back of a wooden spoon.

Pour into warm prepared jars. Cover, seal and label. Keeps up to 2 weeks in fridge. **Makes 675 g/1½ lb**

Strawberry jam

Power setting Full
Total cooking time 32–37 minutes

900 g/2 lb strawberries, hulled
15 g/½ oz citric acid
800 g/1¾ lb (U.S. 3½ cups) granulated sugar

Place the strawberries and citric acid in a large heatproof bowl. Cook until the fruit is very soft, about 12 minutes. Stir in the sugar and mix well. Cook until setting point is reached, about 20–25 minutes. Test for setting every 10 minutes. Leave to stand for 20 minutes before potting, sealing and labelling. **Makes 1.5 kg/3 lb**

Variations
Raspberry jam Prepare as above but use 900 g/2 lb hulled raspberries. **Total cooking time 32–37 minutes**
Gooseberry jam Prepare as above but use 900 g/2 lb topped and tailed gooseberries (U.S. 5 cups stemmed and headed gooseberries). Omit the citric acid and initially cook for 15 minutes to soften the fruit. **Total cooking time 35–40 minutes**

Marmalade

Power setting Full
Total cooking time 50–60 minutes

2 lemons
2 oranges
2 grapefruit
900 ml/1½ pints (U.S. 3¾ cups) boiling water
1.8 kg/4 lb (U.S. 8 cups) granulated sugar

Squeeze the juice from the lemons, oranges and grapefruit. Cut away the peel and shred coarsely into thin strips. Place the remaining pith and any pips in a small piece of muslin and tie to make a small bag.

Place the fruit juices, the muslin bag and strips of peel in a large heatproof bowl. Add 300 ml/½ pint (U.S. 1¼ cups) of the water and leave to marinate for 30 minutes.

Add the remaining boiling water, cover with cling film and cook for 25 minutes. Remove the cling film and stir in the sugar, mixing well. Cook, uncovered, for a further 25–35 minutes or until setting point is reached, stirring every 5 minutes. Test for setting during the last 10 minutes of the cooking time. Leave to stand for 5 minutes before potting, sealing and labelling. **Makes 2.25–2.75 kg/5–6 lb**

Rhubarb chutney

Power setting Full
Total cooking time 30 minutes

450 g/1 lb rhubarb, trimmed and sliced
50 g/2 oz (U.S. $\frac{1}{3}$ cup) raisins
50 g/2 oz sultanas (U.S. $\frac{1}{3}$ cup seedless white raisins)
4 cloves
4 onions, peeled and chopped
150 g/5 oz (U.S. $\frac{3}{4}$ cup) soft brown sugar
$\frac{1}{4}$ teaspoon dry mustard powder
$\frac{1}{4}$ teaspoon salt
grated rind of 1 orange
450 ml/$\frac{3}{4}$ pint (U.S. 2 cups) vinegar

Place the rhubarb in a large heatproof bowl with the raisins, sultanas, cloves, onions, sugar, mustard, salt, orange rind and vinegar. Cover and cook for 30 minutes, stirring every 5 minutes. Ladle into warm prepared jars while still hot. Cover, seal and label. **Makes 900 g/2 lb**

Spicy hot chutney

Power setting Full
Total cooking time 10 minutes

450 g/1 lb (U.S. 4 cups) cooking apples, peeled, cored and chopped
1 onion, peeled and chopped
1 clove garlic, crushed
25 g/1 oz (U.S. 1–2 tablespoons) salt
225 g/8 oz (U.S. 1$\frac{1}{3}$ cups) brown sugar
375 ml/13 fl oz (U.S. 1$\frac{1}{2}$ cups) vinegar
225 g/8 oz (U.S. 1$\frac{1}{2}$ cups) raisins
20 g/$\frac{3}{4}$ oz (U.S. 2–3 tablespoons) ground ginger
20 g/$\frac{3}{4}$ oz (U.S. 2–3 tablespoons) dry mustard powder
$\frac{1}{2}$ teaspoon cayenne pepper

Place the apples, onion, garlic, salt, sugar and vinegar in a bowl, mixing well. Cover with cling film and cook for 10 minutes. Purée in a blender until smooth.

Add the raisins, ginger, mustard and cayenne, blending well. Cover and leave for 8 hours before potting, sealing and labelling. **Makes 900 g/2 lb**

Mustard mango chutney

Power setting Full
Total cooking time about 30–40 minutes

6 ripe mangoes
1 onion, peeled and chopped
450 g/1 lb (U.S. 2$\frac{1}{2}$ cups) brown sugar
600 ml/1 pint (U.S. 2$\frac{1}{2}$ cups) malt vinegar
2 tablespoons (U.S. 3 tablespoons) dry mustard powder
1 tablespoon salt
3 cloves garlic, crushed
2 chillies, seeds removed and chopped

Peel the mangoes and slice thickly. Place in a large bowl with the onion, sugar, vinegar, mustard, salt, garlic and chillies. Cover and bring to the boil, about 10 minutes.

Stir and cook, uncovered, for 20–30 minutes until thick and of the required consistency. Leave to stand for 5 minutes before placing in warm prepared jars with vinegar-proof lids.

Serve with cheese and meat. **Makes 900 ml/1$\frac{1}{2}$ pints (U.S. 3$\frac{3}{4}$ cups)**

Apple and onion pickle

Power setting Full
Total cooking time 3$\frac{1}{2}$–4 minutes

1 kg/2 lb (U.S. 8 cups) cooking apples, peeled, cored and chopped
8 tablespoons (U.S. $\frac{2}{3}$ cup) dried sliced onions
50 g/2 oz (U.S. $\frac{1}{3}$ cup) raisins
4 small hot red chillies
1 tablespoon salt
4 tablespoons (U.S. $\frac{1}{3}$ cup) sugar
25 g/1 oz (U.S. $\frac{1}{4}$ cup) pickling spice
300 ml/$\frac{1}{2}$ pint (U.S. 1$\frac{1}{4}$ cups) white vinegar

Heat four 450-g/1-lb jars with vinegar-proof lids by filling them with boiling water. Drain when hot.

Mix the apples with the onions and raisins. Pack into the prepared hot jars. Bury a hot red chilli in each jar. Place the salt, sugar, spice and vinegar in a bowl and cook for 3$\frac{1}{2}$–4 minutes until boiling. Pour the hot mixture into the jars. Plunge a skewer 3–4 times to the bottom of the jar to let the vinegar mixture filter down. Leave to cool before potting, sealing and labelling. Store for 3–6 months before eating. **Makes 4 (450-g/1-lb) jars**

Piccalilli

(Illustrated on pages 174–175)

Power setting Full
Total cooking time 29 minutes

1 medium cauliflower, broken into florets
225 g/8 oz (U.S. 2 cups) cucumber, chopped
225 g/8 oz (U.S. ½ lb) green tomatoes, chopped
2 onions, peeled and sliced
1 small marrow, chopped (U.S. 1 small squash or zucchini, chopped)
225 g/8 oz (U.S. 2 cups) celery, chopped
16 French beans, trimmed
1.15 litres/2 pints (U.S. 2½ pints) water
25 g/1 oz (U.S. about 1 tablespoon) salt
600 ml/1 pint (U.S. 2½ cups) vinegar
pinch of chilli powder
pinch of allspice
pinch of ground cinnamon
25 g/1 oz plain flour (U.S. ¼ cup all-purpose flour)
2 teaspoons dry mustard powder
¼ teaspoon turmeric
75 g/3 oz (U.S. 6 tablespoons) sugar

Place the cauliflower, cucumber, tomatoes, onions, marrow, celery and beans in a large bowl. Cover with the water and salt and leave for at least 8 hours.

Meanwhile place the vinegar, chilli powder, allspice and cinnamon in a jug and cook for 8 minutes. Allow to cool.

Drain and rinse the vegetables and place in a large bowl. Cover and cook for 5 minutes.

Mix the flour with the mustard powder, turmeric and sugar. Add a little of the vinegar mixture to make a thick paste. Cook the remaining vinegar for 2 minutes until hot. Pour onto the spice paste, mixing well. Cook for 2 minutes, stirring every ½ minute.

Add to the vegetables and stir well to mix and coat. Cover and cook for 12 minutes, stirring every 4 minutes. Leave to stand for 10 minutes before potting, sealing and labelling. **Makes 1.5 kg/3 lb**

Peach and pineapple conserve

Power setting Full
Total cooking time 34 minutes

4 peaches, stoned and sliced (U.S. 4 peaches, pitted and sliced)
1 medium fresh pineapple, peeled, cored and chopped
800 g/1¾ lb (U.S. 3½ cups) granulated sugar

Place the peaches and pineapple in a large heatproof bowl. Cook until the fruit is very soft, about 14 minutes. Stir in the sugar and mix well. Cook for 20 minutes. Leave to stand for 10 minutes before potting, sealing and labelling. **Makes 900 g/2 lb**

Preserved strawberries

(Illustrated on pages 174–175)

Power setting Full
Total cooking time 18–22 minutes

900 g/2 lb strawberries, hulled
1.5 kg/3 lb (U.S. 6 cups) granulated sugar
3 tablespoons (U.S. ¼ cup) lemon juice

Place the strawberries in a heatproof bowl and toss with the sugar. Cover and leave to marinate for at least 8 hours.

Add the lemon juice, blending well. Cook, uncovered, for 10–14 minutes, stirring every 4 minutes until the mixture boils. Cook for a further 8 minutes until thick and syrupy. Leave to stand for 10 minutes before potting, sealing and labelling. **Makes 1.8 kg/4 lb**

Honey and nut brittle

Power setting Full
Total cooking time 8–11 minutes

225 g/8 oz (U.S. 1 cup) sugar
6 tablespoons (U.S. ½ cup) clear honey
200 g/7 oz (U.S. 1⅔ cups) shelled toasted almonds, chopped
7 g/¼ oz (U.S. ½ tablespoon) butter
1 teaspoon baking powder

Place the sugar and honey in a large heatproof bowl and mix well. Cook for 4 minutes. Add the almonds and stir well to blend. Cook for 3–5 minutes or until light brown. Add the butter and cook for 1–2 minutes. Add the baking powder and gently stir until light and foamy.

Pour onto a lightly greased tray and leave until set. Break to serve. **Makes about 12 pieces**

Creamy honey fudge

Power setting Full and Medium/High
Total cooking time 18–20 minutes

450 g/1 lb (U.S. 2 cups) sugar
6 tablespoons (U.S. ½ cup) set or creamed honey
1 (170-g/6-oz) can evaporated milk
50 g/2 oz (U.S. ¼ cup) butter

Place the sugar, honey and evaporated milk in a large heatproof bowl. Cover and cook on *Full Power* for 6 minutes until hot and bubbly. Stir thoroughly and cook on *Medium/High Power*, uncovered, for 12–14 minutes, stirring every 5 minutes. Test to see if the mixture forms a soft ball when a few drops of the mixture are dropped into a cup of cold water. Add the butter and cool until lukewarm.

When almost cold, beat until thick. Pour into a greased 18-cm/7-inch square dish or tin. Mark into 2.5-cm/1-inch squares and leave until set. **Makes 49 pieces**

Gaelic coffee

Power setting Full
Total cooking time 1½–2 minutes

1 measure Irish whiskey
2 teaspoons brown sugar
175 ml/6 fl oz (U.S. ¾ cup) strong brewed coffee
1½ tablespoons double cream (U.S. 2 tablespoons heavy cream)

Place the whiskey, sugar and coffee in a gaelic coffee glass or heatproof tumbler. Cook for 1½–2 minutes until piping hot. Stir well to mix.
Whip the cream lightly then pour over the back of a spoon onto the top of the coffee to make a separate layer. Serve immediately. **Serves 1**

Chocolate marshmallow floats

Power setting Full
Total cooking time 5 minutes

750 ml/1¼ pints (U.S. 3 cups) milk
3 tablespoons (U.S. ¼ cup) drinking chocolate powder
8 marshmallows

Place the milk in a large jug and cook for 5 minutes until just boiling. Quickly whisk in the drinking chocolate, blending well.
Pour into four small heatproof glasses or mugs and top each with two of the marshmallows so that they float. Serve immediately. **Serves 4**

Coffee rum warmer

Power setting Full
Total cooking time $3\frac{1}{2}$–4 minutes

450 ml/¾ pint (U.S. 2 cups) milk
1 large/size 1, 2 egg yolk
3 teaspoons brown sugar
1½ tablespoons (U.S. 2 tablespoons) instant coffee granules
2 measures dark brown rum

Place the milk, egg yolk and sugar in a jug. Cook for 2 minutes. Stir briskly and cook for 1 minute. Add the coffee granules, blending well. Cook for $\frac{1}{2}$–1 minute until piping hot. Stir in the rum and pour into two heatproof glasses. Serve immediately. **Serves 2**

Mocha soother

Power setting Full
Total cooking time $3\frac{1}{2}$–4 minutes

450 ml/¾ pint (U.S. 2 cups) milk
3 teaspoons brown sugar
3 teaspoons cocoa powder (U.S. 3 teaspoons unsweetened cocoa)
2 teaspoons instant coffee granules
2 measures rum
4 tablespoons double cream (U.S. ⅓ cup heavy cream)
½ teaspoon ground nutmeg

Place the milk and sugar in a jug. Cook for 3 minutes. Stir in the cocoa powder and coffee granules, blending well. Cook for $\frac{1}{2}$–1 minute until piping hot. Stir in the rum and pour into two heatproof glasses. Whip the cream lightly then pour over the back of a spoon onto the top of the coffee to make a separate layer. Serve immediately sprinkled with the nutmeg. **Serves 2**

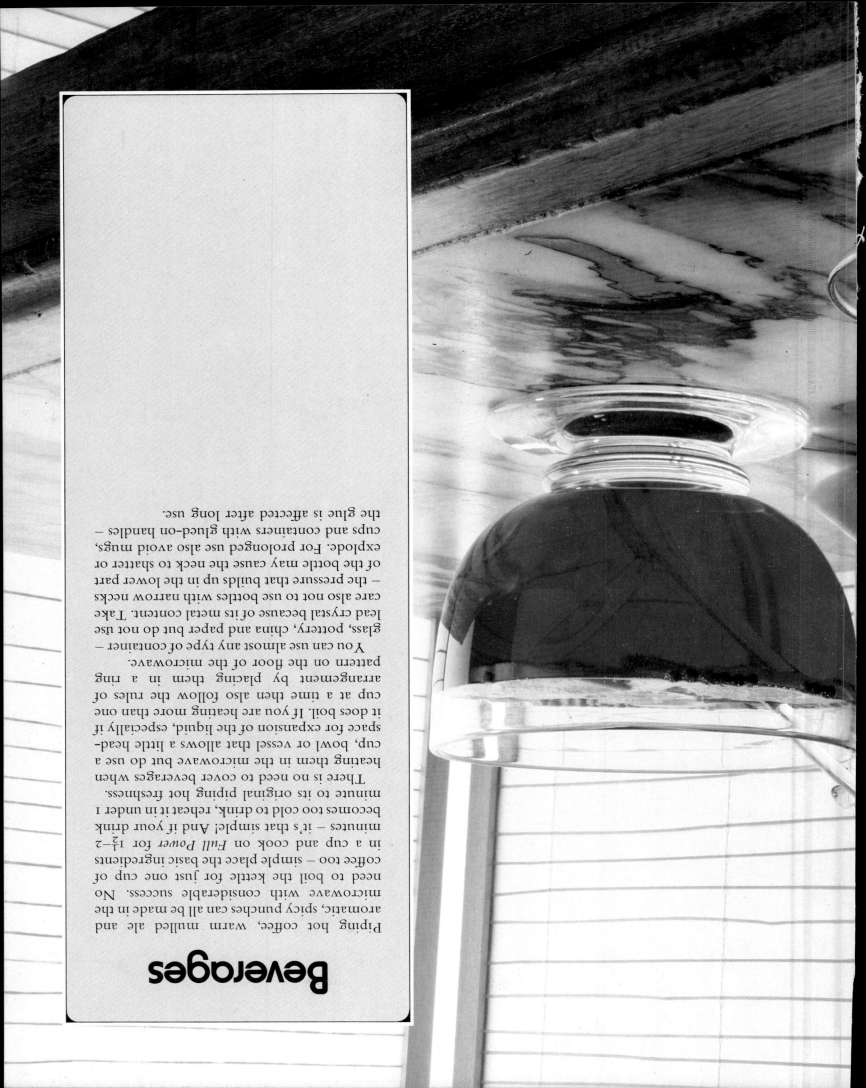

Beverages

Piping hot coffee, warm mulled ale and aromatic, spicy punches can all be made in the microwave with considerable success. No need to boil the kettle for just one cup of coffee too – simple place the basic ingredients in a cup and cook on *Full Power* for 1½–2 minutes – it's that simple! And if your drink becomes too cold to drink, reheat it in under 1 minute to its original piping hot freshness.

There is no need to cover beverages when heating them in the microwave but do use a cup, bowl or vessel that allows a little head-space for expansion of the liquid, especially if it does boil. If you are heating more than one cup at a time then also follow the rules of arrangement by placing them in a ring pattern on the floor of the microwave.

You can use almost any type of container – glass, pottery, china and paper but do not use lead crystal because of its metal content. Take care also not to use bottles with narrow necks – the pressure that builds up in the lower part of the bottle may cause the neck to shatter or explode. For prolonged use also avoid mugs, cups and containers with glued-on handles – the glue is affected after long use.